PC-DOS®/MS-DOS®
SIMPLIFIED

ROD B. SOUTHWORTH

Laramie County Community College

COPYRIGHT 1988
BOYD & FRASER PUBLISHING COMPANY
BOSTON

Programming books from boyd & fraser

Structuring Programs in Microsoft BASIC
BASIC Fundamentals and Style
Applesoft BASIC Fundamentals and Style
Complete BASIC: For the Short Course
Fundamentals of Structured COBOL
Advanced Structured COBOL: Batch and Interactive
Comprehensive Structured COBOL
Pascal
WATFIV-S Fundamentals and Style
VAX Fortran
Fortran 77 Fundamentals and Style
Learning Computer Programming: Structured Logic, Algorithms, and Flowcharting
Structured BASIC Fundamentals and Style for the IBM® PC and Compatibles
C Programming
dBASE III PLUS® Programming

Also available from boyd & fraser

Database Systems: Management and Design
Using Pascal: An Introduction to Computer Science I
Using Modula-2: An Introduction to Computer Science I
Data Abstraction and Structures: An Introduction to Computer Science II
Fundamentals of Systems Analysis with Application Design
Data Communications for Business
Data Communications Software Design
Microcomputer Applications: Using Small Systems Software
The Art of Using Computers
Using Microcomputers: A Hands-On Introduction
A Practical Approach to Operating Systems
Microcomputer Database Management Using dBASE III PLUS®
Microcomputer Database Management Using R:BASE System V®
Office Automation: An Information Systems Approach
Microcomputer Applications: Using Small Systems Software, Second Edition
Mastering Lotus 1-2-3®
Using Enable™: An Introduction to Integrated Software
PC-DOS®/MS-DOS® Simplified
ARTIFICIAL INTELLIGENCE: A Knowledge-Based Approach

Shelly, Cashman, and Forsythe books from boyd & fraser

Computer Fundamentals with Application Software
Workbook and Study Guide to accompany Computer Fundamentals with Application Software
Learning to Use SUPERCALC®3, dBASE III®, and WORDSTAR® 3.3: An Introduction
Learning to Use SUPERCALC®3: An Introduction
Learning to Use dBASE III®: An Introduction
Learning to Use WORDSTAR® 3.3: An Introduction
BASIC Programming for the IBM® Personal Computer
Workbook and Study Guide to accompany BASIC Programming for the IBM® Personal Computer
Structured COBOL — Flowchart Edition
Structured COBOL — Pseudocode Edition
Turbo Pascal Programming

PC-DOS®/MS-DOS®
SIMPLIFIED

CREDITS:

Publisher: Tom Walker
Editor: Pat Donegan
Production Coordinator: Donna Villanucci
Director of Production: Becky Herrington
Director of Manufacturing: Erek Smith
Composition: Erick & Sons
Cover Photography: Mark Wiklund

© 1988 by Boyd & Fraser.

All rights reserved. No part of this work may be reproduced or used in any form or by any means—graphic, electronic, or mechanical, including photocopying, recording, taping, or information and retrieval systems—without written permission from the publisher.

Manufactured in the United States of America

MS-DOS is a registered trademark of Microsoft Corporation.
PC-DOS is a registered trademark of IBM Corporation.

Library of Congress Cataloging-in-Publication Data

```
Southworth, Rod B., 1941-
   PC-DOS/MS-DOS simplified.

   Includes index.
   1. PC DOS (Computer operating system)
2. MS-DOS (Computer operating system)  I. Title.
QA76.76.063S66   1988       005.4'46     88-2829
ISBN 0-87835-308-9
```

4 5 6 7 B 3 2 1 0 9

Contents

PREFACE vii
OBJECTIVES OF THIS BOOK vii
DISTINGUISHING FEATURES viii
ACKNOWLEGDGEMENTS x

CHAPTER 1 INTRODUCTION TO MICROCOMPUTERS 1
HARDWARE 3
SOFTWARE .11
FIRMWARE .12

CHAPTER 2 INTRODUCTION TO DOS 17
BASIC DOS FUNCTIONS 20
SAVING FILES WITH DOS 22
BOOTING DOS 24
FUNDAMENTAL DOS COMMAND CONCEPTS . . .26
FORMATTING DISKS WITH DOS 34

CHAPTER 3 INTERNAL FLOPPY DISK COMMANDS 43
DOS INTERNAL COMMANDS 47

CHAPTER 4 EXTERNAL FLOPPY DISK COMMANDS 61
DOS EXTERNAL COMMANDS 63

CHAPTER 5 FIVE IMPORTANT CONCEPTS 75
BATCH FILES 77
REDIRECTION 82
PIPING 83
EDLIN 85
DOS EDITING KEYS 88

CHAPTER 6 FIXED DISK CONCEPTS AND COMMANDS 99
DIRECTORIES AND SUBDIRECTORIES 102
FIXED DISK COMMANDS 104

CHAPTER 7 ADVANCED COMMANDS 115
ADVANCED DOS COMMANDS 117

APPENDIX A SUMMARY OF DOS COMMANDS 131

APPENDIX B UTILITY SUPPORT PROGRAMS 137

INDEX 143

Preface

This book is recommended for use in any educational or training environment, or for self-study. It was developed with the one-credit PC-DOS/MS-DOS course in mind, but is equally appropriate for use as a supplementary text in any course which introduces DOS commands. No previous experience with computers is required in order to use this book.

OBJECTIVES OF THIS BOOK

The objectives of this book are as follows:
- To provide readers with a fundamental overview of the components of microcomputer systems.
- To introduce readers to the concepts of using systems software.
- To simplify the use of high-frequency DOS commands and associated options.
- To improve the reader's overall ability to use microcomputers effectively through minimized keystrokes, improved file organization, and customized execution of computer processes.

DISTINGUISHING FEATURES

Simplifies Using DOS

In order to accommodate the divergent background and expertise of students using this book, topics in this text are developed in a step-by-step manner. By building upon both students' prior experience and carefully constructed examples of DOS in action, this simplified approach helps readers become self-sufficient microcomputer users.

Focus on High-Frequency DOS Commands

This textbook features step-by-step instruction in using the DOS commands and associated options that are most frequently required by microcomputer users. The text is designed to help readers gain control and a better understanding of microcomputers through efficient use of basic DOS options.

Floppy Disk vs. Hard Disk Environments

In keeping with the current trend in microcomputer instruction, this book consistently addresses using MS/PC-DOS in both floppy disk and hard disk environments. Using DOS with two floppy disk drives is also presented in complete detail.

Emphasis of DOS Structure

An overall understanding of the structure of DOS is essential in effective computer use. Through thorough coverage of disk organization, directory management, and file maintenance, the reader will learn to effectively manage the overall computer system with increased efficiency.

Actual Screen Illustrations

Each DOS instruction is fully supported with screen "dumps" which exactly reflect what the users' screen will look like as they execute each target command. These actual screen illustrations provide users with visual verification which details the impact of each operation performed.

Proven Material

The evolution of this text is based on my experience teaching this course, and on the collective experience of the instructors and students who have successfully used this material in class for several semesters, and have shared with me their comments and suggested improvements. Every attempt has been made to preserve the integrity of those elements which proved effective, and to improve upon those which did not.

Instructor's Support Material

An Instructor's Booklet featuring additional student exercises, helpful teaching suggestions, and a selection of class-tested, multiple choice test questions is available for use in conjunction with this text. Instructors may contact Boyd & Fraser in order to obtain this supplementary material.

ACKNOWLEDGEMENTS

This book would not have been possible without the guidance, help, and advice of many supportive individuals. To Mike Michaelson of Palomar College, and to Paul Ross of Millersville University, I offer my sincere thanks for providing valuable criticism and suggested improvements during each phase of the book's development. I wish to thank all my students and colleagues at Laramie County Community College who had faith in my material, and never failed to make valuable comments about what they did and did not like. My thanks to the editorial staff of Boyd & Fraser for their constant encouragement, patience, and understanding. To Peter Gordon, I offer my thanks for his assistance in developing this book. Pat Donegan did an outstanding job as production editor, and deserves my gratitude. Peter Quintiliani and the Erick & Sons staff did a remarkable job producing the text under ambitious time constraints. To all these people, I remain indebted for their efforts on my behalf.

I would especially like to thank my wife Patrice and our daughters for their patience and understanding.

Rod B. Southworth
Cheyenne, Wyoming
January, 1988

Chapter 1

INTRODUCTION TO MICROCOMPUTERS

HARDWARE
    The Central Processing Unit (CPU)
    Bits, Bytes and Words
    Input/Output Devices
    Secondary Storage
SOFTWARE
    Application Software
    Systems Software
FIRMWARE

Chapter 1

INTRODUCTION TO MICROCOMPUTERS

After reading this chapter, you should understand the major components of microcomputer systems. Since students using this text will undoubtedly have varying degrees of computer experience and knowledge, it is important that everyone has an opportunity to reach a common framework of microcomputer concepts and terminology.

All microcomputer systems are comprised of three major parts: hardware, software, and firmware. This chapter discusses each of these parts with the intent of bringing each student to a minimal level of understanding about microcomputer systems. This system knowledge should greatly facilitate both the learning and understanding of either PC-DOS or MS-DOS.

When you purchase a microcomputer system, you may need to make choices related to both the power of the CPU and the types of I/O and storage devices you will want to attach. The level of technical knowledge presented in this chapter will assist you in making the right choices.

HARDWARE

Typically, discussion of **hardware** involves three categories: the Central Processing Unit (CPU), the various Input/Output (I/O) devices, and storage devices. Figure 1-1 summarizes the various hardware parts and categories of microcomputer systems discussed in this chapter.

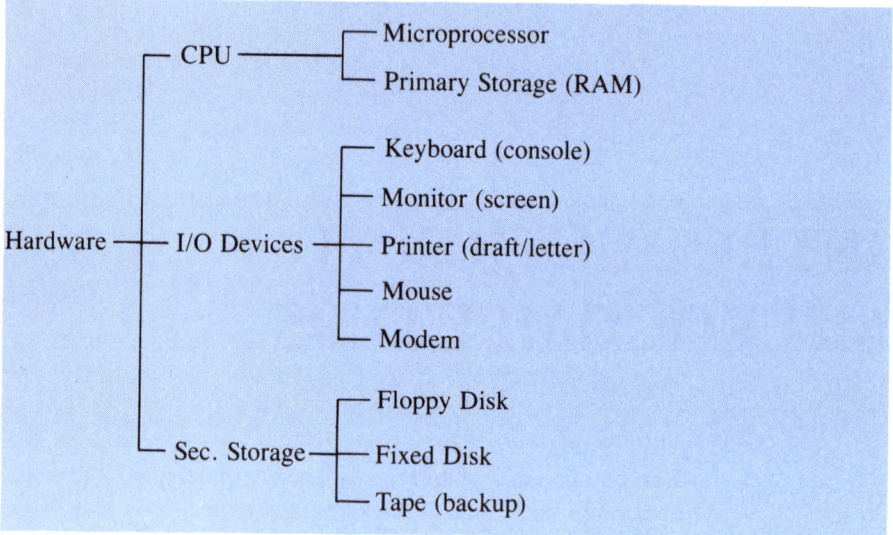

Figure 1-1 Microcomputer Hardware

The Central Processing Unit (CPU)

The **central processing unit**, or CPU, has often been described as the "heart" of a computer system. It is comprised of a **microprocessor** and varying amounts of temporary storage locations referred to as **primary storage**. The CPU is typically organized around one of four microprocessor chips designed by the Intel Corporation: the 8088, 8086, 80286, and 80386. Each of these microprocessor chips have different capabilities, related primarily to speed and overall processing power.

Bits, Bytes and Words

All computer circuits, including microprocessors, function in one of two states: on and off. Symbolically, we represent the on condition by the value 1 and the off condition by the value 0. These two values are binary digits, or bits. A grouping of bits can be combined to represent characters that we need to process on a computer. Eight bits are typically grouped together to represent characters, where a character is a number (0-9), an alphabetic letter (A-Z), or a special symbol, such as an asterisk, dollar sign, decimal point, etc. For example, the bit pattern 10000001 might represent the letter A.

When each group of 8 bits is individually addressable, it is called a byte. Most of the earlier computers were "byte machines." However, it is generally more efficient to access and work with more than one character at a time. When bytes are grouped (always in multiples of 2), the addressable groups are called words. A 16-bit word represents 2 characters, a 32 bit word represents 4 characters and so on. Word machines access and transfer characters faster than byte machines.

The 8088 microprocessor is the most common of the four chips. It has a 16-bit internal word structure with an 8-bit path for input and output. The 8086 is a similar chip, but with a 16-bit path for input and output, which allows for faster transfer of data between the CPU and I/O devices.

All microprocessor chips use a **clock rate** that determines the frequency of the internal operations and keeps everything under control. The faster the clock runs, the faster the computer can process data and instructions. Clock rates are measured in units called **megahertz**, a term for one million cycles per second. The internal clock speed of both the 8088 and 8086 chip is 4.77 megahertz (MHz).

The 80286 microprocessor has a 32-bit internal word length, with a 16-bit I/O path. Its internal clock is rated at 8-12 MHz, making it at least twice as powerful as the older, more common chips previously mentioned. The latest chip, the 80386, is about twice as fast as the 80286, with an internal clock speed of 16-20 MHz. This chip is currently being touted as the chip of the future. But don't get discouraged if you don't have the latest chip. The common chips used today, while not as fast and powerful as the 80386, are more than adequate for most microcomputer applications. When the speed limit is only 55 MPH, a VW bug can be as effective as a racing car.

Primary storage, the second major part of a CPU, is a temporary holding location for both programmed instructions (software) and data to be processed. Therefore, the concepts of storing data apply equally to the storing of software. The number of primary storage locations on microcomputers typically range from 256K to 768K, where K is roughly equivalent to 1000 characters. The microprocessor is responsible for executing software that tells the computer how to process the data in primary storage. These instructions also tell the microprocessor when and where to send data to an output device, such as a printer, as well as when and where to get additional data to be processed.

Primary storage is generally referred to as RAM (Random Access Memory) because the storing of data causes the affected storage locations to be changed and allows for any storage location to be accessed at any time. Data are stored in a given storage location and remain there until new data have replaced it, or until the electricity has been turned off.

Because most RAM chips lose their "memory" when the power is discontinued, primary storage is considered temporary. If you want to permanently save data, you must save it to a secondary storage device, such as magnetic tape or disk.

It is important for microcomputer users to realize the potential damage that static electricity can do to the CPU. The amount of static electricity that you sometimes feel when you touch a doorknob or another person is hundreds of times greater than the static electricity needed to permanently damage a microprocessor or RAM chip. For this reason, precautions should be taken to minimize the potential for static electricity around your microcomputer. The computer or computer area can be protected by:

1. placing the computer system in a non-carpeted area,
2. keeping the computer area at relative humidity of about 45% or more,
3. using a static spray on fabrics, and
4. employing a static mat and good computer grounding to discharge static electricity harmlessly into the electrical system.

Input/Output Devices

Input/Output devices are the means by which you enter data into the computer (input) or view data you have previously entered (output).

The Keyboard

The keyboard on a personal computer is an input device similar to a typewriter keyboard, except it has additional special keys. The IBM-PC and IBM-compatible keyboard have over 80 keys (see Figure 1-2) and may vary somewhat among manufacturers. A good understanding of the keyboard is essential when working with DOS.

PC-DOS/MS-DOS SIMPLIFIED   7

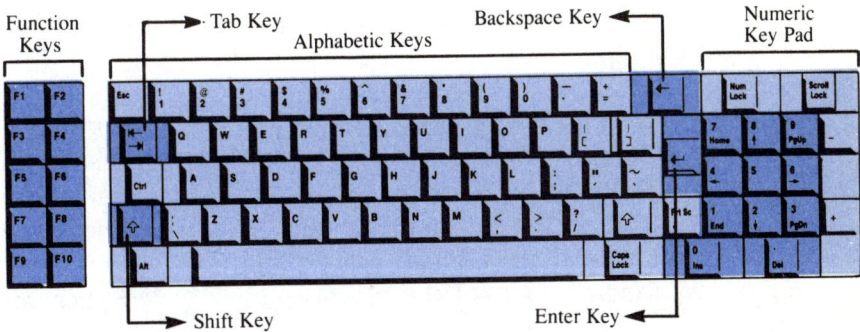

Figure 1-2 Keyboard

A set of 10 keys, usually on the left side and labeled F1 through F10, are called **function keys**. These "programmable" keys serve different functions depending on how the software has been programmed to use them. Any time reference to a function key is made in this text, or in the DOS Manual, it will generally be referred to by the key name, such as the F1 key, or the F6 key.

The **numeric keypad** is a group of 10 keys, usually located near the right side of the keyboard, containing keys numbered 0-9. It can be used to enter numbers only when the Num Lock key has been activated. The Num Lock key is an example of a "toggle" key, one which acts as a switch. Press it once and the toggle is switched on; press it a second time and it is turned off. Normally, the Num Lock key is "off" and numbers are entered by pressing the numeric keys located on the top row of the keyboard. Another example of a toggle key is the Caps Lock key that shifts all lower case alphabetic characters (a-z) to upper case (A-Z) when switched on.

With the Num Lock key switched off, the numeric keypad keys become arrows that are used to position the cursor on the screen. The **cursor** is a special character, usually a blip or an underline, that identifies a location on the computer screen where the next action or entry of data is to occur.

Some keys must be used in combination with other keys to obtain the desired results. For example, with the exception of the numeric keypad, all keys with both an upper and lower character shown on the key require that the shift key be depressed to enter the upper symbol. For example, in order to enter a "$", you must press the Shift key and the "4" key simultaneously. The Shift key is also used to enter capitalized alphabetic letters without using the Caps Lock key. Some of the more important keys used in combination and their functions are shown in Figure 1-3. (Note that the Break key is sometimes shown as Scroll Lock.)

Combination Keys	Function
Control + Break (Ctrl-Brk)	Break execution
Control + "S" (Ctrl-S)	Pause screen
Shift + Print Screen (Shift-PrtSc)	Print current screen
Control + Print Screen (Ctrl-PrtSc)	Print continuous screen
Control + Alt + Del (Ctrl-Alt-Del)	System reset (warm boot)

Figure 1-3 Combination Keys

As you enter commands from a keyboard, you can use the Backspace key, normally shown as a large left-facing arrow (←), to backspace and erase unwanted characters. The backspace key erases one character at a time each time it is pressed.

Once a command has been keyed completely, it must be sent to the computer, or entered, by pressing the **Enter key**. The Enter key, sometimes referred to as the Return key, is normally located near the right side of the keyboard, just to the left of the numeric keypad. On most keyboards it is shown as a bent left-facing arrow (↵).

Since modern keyboards are electronic and not mechanical, a very light touch is all that is required to activate the keys. If you continue to hold down a key, the keyboard will repeat that keystroke until you release the key. This is known as the "repeating" key concept and may cause problems for you initially.

In computer terminology, a **buffer** is a holding area that can temporarily store a limited number of computer characters. The keyboard has a buffer that allows it to retain keystrokes until the program you are using has "caught up" with you. If you are an extremely fast typist, or are using a program that processes keystrokes slower than you are entering them, the buffer can save them until they are needed. Thus, as you type, some keystrokes will not be automatically "echoed" on the screen, as they may still be in the buffer.

The Monitor

In addition to requiring the use of a keyboard, personal computers need a **monitor** (screen) to communicate with the user. Keystrokes entered from the keyboard are echoed on the screen to provide visual verification. When the computer wants to communicate with you, it displays data, error messages, and system prompts on the screen. Most monitors display up to 80 characters of text on the screen. There are three basic categories of monitors: **monochrome**, **composite color**, and **RGB (Red-Green-Blue) color monitors**. Monochrome monitors are limited to a single color, usually amber, green, or white, and are suitable for most applications. If your application requires multiple colors or graphics, then you will probably need a color monitor. The composite color monitor is less expensive than the RGB color monitor, but not as popular, probably due to the fact that the RGB color monitors generate a significantly better color image than the composite color monitors.

The sharpness and clarity of images on the screen are directly related to the **screen resolution**. The higher the resolution, the sharper the image. Low-resolution monitors display about 320 x 200 picture elements (pixels) on the screen, or about 320 dots horizontally and 200 dots vertically. Pixels are locations on the screen that can be lit as required. Medium-resolution monitors, like most IBM-PCs, typically have 640 x 200 or 720 x 350 pixels. High-resolution monitors, like those used by engineers for computer graphics, may go as high as 1024 x 1024 pixels. Images displayed on a screen are termed softcopy because they are only temporary. Permanent images, called **hardcopy**, require the use of a printer.

The Printer

Printers for microcomputers are generally classified as one of two types: letter-quality or draft-quality (dot matrix). **Letter-quality printers**, which print documents that look like they were created by a typewriter, typically create each character by striking a fully-formed image of a character against an inked ribbon and paper. **Draft-quality printers**, which produce images of a lesser quality, sufficient for most applications, use a dot matrix technique that creates a pattern of dots to represent each character or image. Many dot matrix printers can produce "near letter-quality" output by reprinting each character, adding additional dots to fill in the image with a denser pattern of dots. The printing of additional dots tends to cut printing speeds by half or more. As a general rule, dot matrix printers are faster and less expensive than letter-quality printers. In addition, dot matrix printers are more flexible in that they can print a wide variety of patterns, including numerous graphic images.

The Mouse

A number of microcomputers, including the IBM-PC family, allow for a **mouse** to be attached as an input device. The mouse is a pointing device. As you move the mouse across a flat surface, it relays information to the computer that moves the cursor in various directions. Once the mouse is positioned, you can press a button on the mouse to inform the computer you have moved the cursor to its destination. A mouse allows you to quickly and easily select options on the screen. However, you need software that supports a mouse before you can use it to control the cursor.

The Modem

You may have a need to communicate with other computers via telephone lines. For computers to send and receive data over the telephone, they must use a **modem** to convert the computer's digital signals to the analog signals used by telephones, and vice versa. Modems can be internal (located inside the computer), or they can be external. The speed with which the modem can send and receive data is known as its **baud rate**. The higher the baud rate, the less time (and so, less money) it takes to transmit and receive data. Common baud rates are 1200 and 2400, where 1200 baud is roughly equivalent to 120 characters per second.

The I/O Interface

Any input/output device attached to a CPU must have some type of control unit to allow it to interact with the CPU and make the appropriate translations between each I/O device and the CPU. These control units are often referred to as **interface boards** or **cards**. They consist of a sturdy card containing electronic chips. Sometimes static electricity, or some other power-related problem, will cause these chips to fail and they may have to be replaced if damaged.

These cards are relatively easy to remove because they plug directly into slots on the CPU's system board. The number of slots available depends on the system board. Most system boards have slots for a keyboard, a monitor, a serial device (like a mouse or joystick), a parallel device (like a printer), a modem, and one or more disk drives. Since the number of slots are limited, manufacturers have developed multifunction boards, which combine two or more tasks. Some of the functions typically combined on multifunction boards include: additional primary storage, a clock and battery to set the computer's clock when the computer is initially turned on, a parallel port to connect a printer, an RS-232 serial port to connect serial devices like a mouse or modem, and a game adapter port to connect a joystick.

Secondary Storage

When you create data on a computer or write programs, you cannot save them permanently in RAM (Random Access Memory), the computer's primary storage area. RAM is not nearly large enough to store even a modest number of files containing data and/or programs. Secondary storage facilities are required to store a potentially unlimited amount of data on a permanent basis. Secondary storage costs per bit stored are considerably less than primary storage costs. Microcomputers support three typical classifications of secondary storage devices: floppy disks, fixed disks, and magnetic tape.

Floppy Disks

Floppy disks are the most common medium for secondary storage and come in various sizes. The most common size for the IBM-PC family of personal computers is 5 1/4 inch disks each of which can contain up to 360,000 characters (bytes) of data. (This is usually shown as 360KB, where KB represents roughly one thousand bytes.) These disks allow data to be written in "double density," or on 40 tracks per side, using both sides of the disk for storage. Certain of the 5 1/4 inch disks, called high density disks, can hold up to 1,200,000 bytes (1-2 megabytes) of data.

When you insert a floppy disk into a floppy disk drive and close the latch, the disk is secured by two clamps that close on the large center hole of the disk. When data is to be either read from or written to the disk, a motor connected to the clamps spins the disk inside its outer jacket at 300 rpm, about ten times faster than a 33 1/3 album spins on a record turntable. A small red light on the disk drive indicates when the drive is spinning, so you will know not to attempt to remove the disk. The newer and smaller 3 1/2 inch disks use improved technology to record 720KB of data. PC-DOS Version 3.2 will support the new disks, whereas the older versions will not.

Floppy disks are not completely reliable because they can be damaged. However, if you take proper care of them, floppy disks can serve you faithfully for a long time. Figure 1-4 contains some helpful and very important tips for the "care and feeding" of floppies.

1. Store floppies in their protective covers when not in use.
2. Store them vertically to minimize chances of warping.
3. Shade them from direct sunlight or intense heat.
4. Write on any attached labels with felt tip pens only.
5. Never touch the recording surface of a floppy disk.
6. Never bend, fold, or otherwise mutilate a floppy disk.
7. Keep the disk clean from contaminants, including smoke.
8. Do not attempt to clean the surface of a disk.
9. Never place a disk near a magnetic field or magnets.

Figure 1-4 Proper Care of Floppy Disks

Fixed Disks

Fixed disks have a significant advantage over floppy disks in that they are roughly 20 times faster to use. When the fixed disk drive is operating, it spins at 3600 rpm, or twelve times faster than a floppy disk. In addition, you do not have to be continually swapping disks, since fixed disks will typically hold 10, 20, or 40 megabytes of data. [A megabyte (MB) is equivalent to one million characters of storage.] Fixed disks can store data using a much higher density than floppy disks because they use rigid metal platters in a sealed environment. A 20MB fixed disk can store the equivalent of fifty-six 360KB floppy disks.

It is not practical for personal computers to have only a fixed disk drive installed, however. Floppy disks are used extensively for transferring data and programs from one computer to another, and for backup so it is ideal to have one fixed and one floppy drive. In addition, because of the vast amount of data files that can be stored on most fixed disk systems, it is important to establish appropriate file naming conventions, a topic covered in Chapter 2.

Magnetic Tape

The last medium of secondary storage is magnetic tape. Since this medium only allows for sequential retrieval of data, it is not appropriate for most applications. Because magnetic tape is significantly less expensive than disks (per unit stored), it makes an ideal medium for storing historical or backup data. Large businesses typically use one of their expansion slots on the system board to connect a high-speed tape drive to be used solely for backup.

SOFTWARE

In addition to hardware, a computer system must have **software** to control and operate the hardware. Figure 1-5 depicts the various classifications of software required.

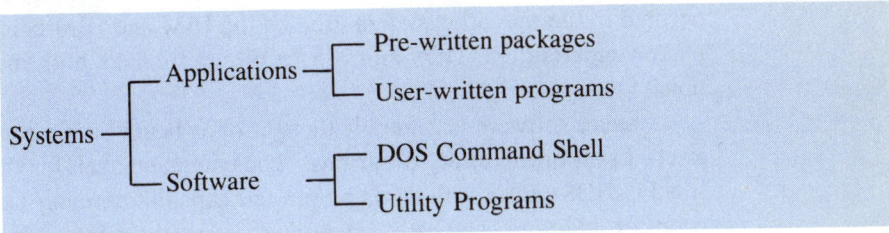

Figure 1-5 Microcomputer Software

Application Software

Application software is written for a specific purpose, such as inventory, word processing, or payroll. It can be created by the user at great expense and time, or it can be purchased outright. It is not recommended that novice users attempt to write their own application software; it takes a great deal of skill to be able to write reasonably productive software. Furthermore, the cost of prewritten programs is relatively cheap and the development costs are shared with hundreds, even thousands, of users.

When you purchase individual application programs, it would be helpful if they were **integrated**—in other words, provide several applications in one package. Integration provides two major benefits. Generally, learning how to operate the programs is easier, since commands are usually similar with integrated packages. In addition, you have transferability of data between a variety of integrated applications—say, between a spreadsheet and a word processor—which saves duplication of effort.

Systems Software

Your computer system needs **systems software** to act as an interface between the application programs and the hardware. The two major functions of a computer's operating system are to control the computer's operations and to manage files. The operating system allows you to use the computer in either an interactive mode or a batch mode. **Interactive processing** is normally characterized by the user entering a command, followed by the computer executing that command, and then the user issuing yet another command when the computer has finished the previous one. **Batch processing** typically occurs when a user has issued a series of commands, previously stored in the computer, that the operating system will execute whenever it is ready. The next chapter is devoted to the operating system used by the IBM and IBM-compatible family of microcomputers (PC-DOS and MS-DOS), and covers both methods of operations.

Systems software is generally thought of as being both a **command shell** and a set of supporting **utility programs**. The command shell for the IBM-PC family is PC-DOS. Even with all its power and capabilities, many users have found a need for additional software, primarily to assist them in making DOS friendlier (easier to use) and more powerful, so they turn to utility programs, such as the ever-popular SideKick. Some utility programs can be executed at any time, even in the middle of executing another program. Numerous utility programs are devoted to improving upon DOS. Examples of these programs include Microsoft Windows, 1dir+, Norton Utilities, PC-Tools, and Fastback, to name just a few. Appendix B discusses utility support programs and provides more detailed examples.

FIRMWARE

The last topic that we should mention before delving into DOS is the use of **firmware** by microcomputers. Firmware is defined as "software contained in the form of hardware." This hardware, used to store preprogrammed instructions, is called **ROM** (Read-only Memory). Special-purpose programs are built into ROM chips during manufacturing. Since programs stored in ROM are "burned into" computer memory, they are available to be executed without having to be specifically loaded into RAM. ROM is a form of non-volatile memory in that it does not lose its memory when the power is turned off like RAM. Therefore, ROM is often used to hold operating system startup programs and language translators, such as BASIC.

When you turn on your computer system, a ROM chip automatically tests the hardware for problems and then reads a disk in order to load DOS. If you have an IBM-PC (not one of the many IBM clones or compatibles), the instructions for interpreting BASIC programs are contained on a proprietary ROM chip. In the future, more and more software will be available in the form of inexpensive ROM chips. Currently, laptop and other "portable" microcomputers contain both the operating system and several application programs in ROM.

Review Questions for Chapter 1

1. What are the three major parts of a microcomputer?
2. What is the major difference between primary storage and secondary storage?
3. What is the major difference between RAM and ROM?
4. What is the purpose of a clock rate in a microprocessor?
5. What is the potential danger of static electricity?
6. What is the purpose of function keys?
7. What is meant by the term "toggle key"?
8. Give two examples of toggle keys on the keyboard.
9. What keys must be pressed to halt execution of an operation?
10. What happens when you press the backspace key (the one with the large backarrow)?
11. What is the repeating key concept?
12. What term is used to define the sharpness and clarity of images on the display screen?
13. What is the difference between hardcopy and softcopy?
14. What are some advantages that dot matrix printers have over letter-quality printers?
15. What is the most common form of secondary storage on micros?
16. What are the major differences between fixed disks and floppy disks?

17. What is the difference between application software and systems software?
18. What are the major benefits of utility support programs?
19. What is the difference between batch processing and interactive processing on microcomputers?
20. What are the benefits of using integrated software packages?

INTRODUCTION TO DOS

BASIC DOS FUNCTIONS
    Control of Input-Output Operations
    Interpret and Execute Commands
    File Management
SAVING FILES WITH DOS
BOOTING DOS
FUNDAMENTAL DOS COMMAND CONCEPTS
    Default Disk Drive
    Standard Device Names
    File Naming Conventions
    Global Characters
    The Dos Directory Listing
    Internal vs. External Commands
    DOS Versions
FORMATTING DISKS WITH DOS

2
Chapter

INTRODUCTION TO DOS

The primary objective of Chapter 2 is to teach you the basic functions of DOS related to file management and command processing. By the end of this chapter, you will understand such file management techniques as how disks are formatted and how files are saved on disk. In addition to learning how DOS is booted, Chapter 2 will also teach you fundamental DOS command concepts, which include: default disk drive, standard device names, global characters, file naming conventions, and internal vs. external commands. This chapter also will introduce you to four introductory DOS commands: DATE, TIME, DIR, and FORMAT.

An **operating system** is an integral part of all computer systems. It allows users like yourself to conveniently use the computer as a tool. The operating system is a helpful translator between the hardware and either application programs or users, coordinating and controlling all of the activities of the computer (see Figure 2-1).

20   INTRODUCTION TO DOS

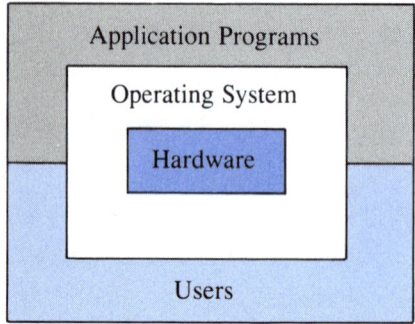

Figure 2-1   The role of an O.S.

The operating system contains a group of commands and programs that allow users to interact directly with the computer. For example, it provides an easy way to copy data from one disk to another, allowing you to conveniently make backup copies of important data.

This chapter introduces you to a specific type of disk operating system (DOS) called PC-DOS (MS-DOS) that is used on both IBM and IBM-compatible microcomputers. Because of the similarities of PC-DOS and MS-DOS, this text will refer to this operating system simply as DOS. When differences occur, then the appropriate term (PC-DOS or MS-DOS) will be used.

BASIC DOS FUNCTIONS

DOS has three major functions. The first controls the input and output operations of your computer. The second function interprets and executes commands that you enter from your keyboard or other input devices. The third major function deals with file management, which allows you to permanently record files on disks and effectively manage them.

Control of Input-Output Operations

All application programs share the same input and output problems. They all have to accept data from the keyboard, display data on the monitor, store data temporarily in main memory, store data permanently on disk, and retrieve data from disks. It requires a great number of instructions to coordinate and control all of these activities on a microcomputer. Without an operating system, each application program would have to duplicate these instructions. On the PC-DOS disk, two "**hidden files**," **IBMDOS.COM and IBMBIO.COM**, provide the input-output instructions required by DOS and by application programs. (They are called hidden files because they do not appear on the directory of files when you attempt to list the files contained on your DOS disk.) IBMDOS.COM provides some common services, like copying files, deleting files, searching directories, and reading the keyboard. IBMBIO.COM contains additions and corrections to the device-handling **BIOS** (Basic Input/Output System) routines that are built into your system on ROM chips. In MS-DOS, the hidden files are typically named MSDOS.SYS and IO.SYS.

Interpret and Execute Commands

The command processor part of DOS interprets and executes the commands that you enter, and interprets and executes commands from application programs as well. Without an operating system, you would have no effective way to communicate with the hardware and direct its activities.

File Management

As a user, you will be heavily involved with the file management role of DOS. For example, before files can be saved on a disk, you must prepare the disk to record files. Then, you can save, rename, copy or delete disk files. DOS provides a series of complex commands to allow both the user and application programs to better manage the multitude of disk files that you will create over a period of time. The subsequent chapters of this book will be primarily devoted to the file management commands provided by DOS.

SAVING FILES WITH DOS

A **file** is a group of related records. Each **record** consists of a **string**, or series, of characters that can be entered and saved as part of a given file. Records consist of either program instructions or data. Thus, files are categorized as either **program files** or **data files**.

Saving files on disk is a requirement of all operating systems. The files you create and work with in main memory are temporary, and only become permanent when you save them on disk. When you turn off the computer, or otherwise lose power to main memory, all programs and data stored in main memory are destroyed. You can easily save files on disk and recall them when needed. Follow this process to save files on disk:

(1) IBM and IBM-compatible floppy disk drives are double-sided, meaning data can be stored on both sides of the disk. By recording both sides of a disk before moving to another track, recording head movement is minimized and disk access speed is increased. When you issue a save command from an application program or directly from DOS, the operating system reads the directory portion of the appropriate disk to determine a suitable location on the disk to save the file. The area on formatted disks used to record data is comprised of **clusters** that are, in turn, made up of **sectors** and **tracks**. The cluster size on a 360KB floppy is 1024 bytes, as a sector (on any track) always contains 512K bytes, and two sectors make a cluster. Although sector size remains constant, the size of the cluster may vary depending on the disk drive used and the number of read/write heads per track. On fixed disks, cluster sizes typically involve 4 sectors (or about 4K bytes). Large cluster sizes improve performance of disk access when files are large, but may waste space when files are relatively small.

(2) If the file being saved is a new file, DOS will look for an area of the disk that has enough contiguous clusters to hold the file. If the file has been previously saved on that disk, DOS will replace the previous contents of the file with the contents of the current file in main memory. Sometimes the disk begins to fill and the operating system is not able to locate enough adjoining clusters. In that case, it will use noncontiguous clusters to save the data. The additional head movement causes the system to slow down somewhat when writing or retrieving those files.

(3) Whenever a file has been saved, DOS updates the **File Allocation Table (FAT)** on the disk with the appropriate clusters required to permanently store the file. Then it updates the disk directory on the disk with the size of the file, in bytes, and the date/time the file was saved. For this reason, it is important

that the operating system is booted with the correct date and time. The directory will allow up to 512 entries, including filenames (hidden and otherwise) and subdirectory names. (Because subdirectories are normally applicable to fixed disk systems, we will be discuss them later.) The file information stored on a disk directory is as follows:
- filename and filename extension
- file attribute (hidden file, read-only file, backup status)
- date and time of creation or last update
- starting cluster number in FAT
- file size in bytes

BOOTING DOS

Before you can use an operating system, you must load it from a secondary storage device, such as a disk, to the main memory (RAM) of the computer. Since not all of the operating system can be loaded at once, a process known as **booting the system** is used to load the controlling portion of the operating system.

There are two general methods of booting any operating system. One way is called a "cold boot" because the computer is turned off prior to booting the operating system. The second method is termed a "warm boot" because the computer is already turned on and was booted previously, but needs to be rebooted. In both cases, DOS executes the same sets of commands in the boot process.

The major difference between the two types of boots is in how the boot process is initiated. With a cold boot, the computer is simply turned on to initiate the booting process. With the warm boot, you must enter a sequence of three keys simultaneously: the Control key, the Alternate key and the Delete key (**Ctrl-Alt-Del**). It is advisable to use a warm boot whenever possible to minimize the possibility of damaging the computer's chips when the power is turned on. The following steps are executed to boot DOS stored on a floppy disk. (We will discuss booting from a fixed disk in Chapter 6.)

1. Place the disk containing DOS in disk drive A with the latch securely closed. (Drive A is usually either the top drive or leftmost drive in micros with two drives.) Then turn on the power to both the monitor and the CPU.

2. The microcomputer begins executing a small start-up program stored in ROM that instructs it to run some predetermined diagnostic tests. These tests include checking the computer's RAM and keyboard interface to make sure they are functional. If there are any problems, the program will display an appropriate error message on your screen.

3. If the computer passes the diagnostic checks, the program in ROM loads the two DOS hidden files contained on the DOS disk in Drive A. It also loads the file called COMMAND.COM into RAM from Drive A. COMMAND.COM contains many of the DOS commands you will use, and is the primary command interpreter, processor, and loader. Occasionally, another program will require some of the memory occupied by the COMMAND.COM file. When that program is finished, you will be prompted to insert the disk containing COMMAND.COM file in the default drive, so that it can be reloaded.

4. At this point, DOS will accommodate more advanced users by looking for a file on Drive A called AUTOEXEC.BAT. If DOS finds this file, it will execute it immediately. Sophisticated DOS users utilize an AUTOEXEC.BAT file to simplify the booting process by executing a common set of boot-related programs. DOS will also look for an optional CONFIG.SYS file that can be used to specify some of the different ways your system can be configured, or customized. The use of these two files will be explained in later chapters.

5. If there is no AUTOEXEC.BAT file, the system will ask you to enter the correct date and correct time, so that it can keep track of the time with its own internal clock. Once you have entered the date and time, DOS will display the version number of the operating system and will **prompt** you to enter a command. The **default prompt** is A, where the A represents the **default disk drive** (the one containing DOS). Figure 2-2 shows you how the screen might look if you entered in a date of July 4, 1987 and a time of 1:45 PM. The A is the system prompt, which requests the next command; the underline character following it is the cursor. For illustrative purposes, the data you entered is shown in boldface.

> Current date is Tue 1-01-1980
> Enter new date (mm-dd-yy): **07-04-87**
> Current time is 0:01.05.58
> Enter new time: **13:45**
> The IBM Personal Computer DOS
> Vers. 3.10 (C)Copyright International Business Machines 1981, 1985
> (C)Copyright Microsoft Corp 1981, 1985
> A_

Figure 2-2   Display Screen After Booting PC-DOS

The system date is entered using month, day, and year in the form of mm-dd-yy or mm/dd/yy. The system time is always entered using military time, in which the hours are from 0 to 23. Time is entered using hours, minutes, seconds, and hundredths of seconds in the form of hh:mm:ss:hh. (The use of seconds and hundredths of seconds is optional.) You can use either a slash (/), a dash (-), or a period (.) to separate the date entries. You can only use the colon (:) or a period (.) to separate time entries.

As with most operating systems, when you are finished entering a command or some data (like date or time), you need to press the Enter key to let the system know you are finished keying.

If at a later time you wanted to change either the system date or time, all you would need to do is enter a relatively simple command. To change the date, enter **DATE** and press the Enter key. DOS will display the current date for you and tell you to enter a new date. The format of the new date is the same as with the boot process (mm-dd-yy). When entering the date, you do not have to enter leading zeros. For example, the month of February can be entered as 02, or just 2. Also, you do not have to enter the century. For instance, the year 1987 is simply entered as 87. If you change your mind and decide not to change the date, just press the Enter key.

To change the time, enter **TIME** and change it using the same format as the boot process: hh:mm:ss. When entering hours, remember that hours are entered using military time. For example, 8 P.M. is "twenty hundred hours," and is entered as 20.

As long as DOS keeps running, it will keep track of time, automatically changing both the time and the date. Many systems today have a small battery and additional software to keep track of date and time when the computer is turned off. When the system is booted, an AUTOEXEC.BAT file can contain the commands to automatically set the system date and time from this battery operated clock.

FUNDAMENTAL DOS COMMAND CONCEPTS

Before learning specific DOS commands, you need to know the basic concepts common to the majority of DOS commands. Once learned, these concepts can be easily applied to all of the individual commands. The fundamental concepts to be learned include: the use of a default disk drive, standard device names used by DOS, the need for effective file naming conventions, the use of global characters, and the basic types of DOS commands.

Default Disk Drive

Most computer systems have at least two disk drives. If your computer only has a single floppy disk, you will waste a great deal of time swapping floppies in and out of that one drive. If you have at least two drives, then running application programs becomes easier. In many cases, two drives are required.

Most applications require that the program disk be located in one drive and your data disk in another. If you have a fixed disk installed in your computer, then it can easily contain both your application program(s) and your data. However, you would still need at least one floppy disk drive to allow you to load files from floppies to the fixed disk, or to make backup copies of your fixed disk files on floppies.

When running DOS, the system will need to know what disk drive you are specifying in the commands you enter. DOS employs the "default drive technique," a concept that will be referred to often in this text. Fundamental to this concept is that you can specify which of the disk drives is to be the default. Whenever you enter a command that does not contain a disk drive specification, DOS will substitute the default drive for the missing one(s) in the command. By understanding the default drive concept when entering commands, you can save a significant number of keystrokes. Remember, you only need to designate a disk drive if it is other than the default drive.

To identify the different disk drives, DOS uses a coding scheme consisting of alphabetic letters. In most cases the letters "A" and "B" are used for floppy drives, while the letters "C" and "D" are used for fixed disk drives. DOS will establish the initial default drive as the drive that was used to boot the system. You can easily change the default to another drive whenever you wish. When you booted DOS and saw the A prompt, the "A" referred to the default disk drive. This is the system's method of reminding you what drive is the current default drive.

To change the default drive, you need to enter a new disk drive letter followed by a colon. Example: **A>B:**

Entered at the A prompt, this command will change the default drive from A to B. Once entered, the default drive will be the B drive (the second floppy drive) and the system prompt will now be displayed as **B>**.

Standard Device Names

As with most operating systems, DOS reserves some names to represent system devices. For example, when used in DOS commands, the reserved word CON represents the keyboard (console). The reserved words LPT1 and PRN are used to designate the line printer. Printer designations are especially useful when you wish to redirect output that would normally go to the screen to the printer for a hardcopy listing. Since reserved words have a specific meaning to DOS, you should never use them to name a file. Other reserved device names include: AUX1, COM1, COM2, LPTR2, LPTR3, and NUL.

File Naming Conventions

DOS uses a **file specification** to tell it where to search for a specified file. The file specification consists of four parts: the disk drive designator, the path, the filename, and the filename extension. Only the filename itself is required. The other three parts are optional and are shown in brackets as follows:

[d:][path]filename[.ext]

The initial parameter "d:" is used to specify the disk drive. To specify a drive, enter the drive letter followed by a colon. If you omit the drive designator, the default disk drive will be substituted by DOS.

The next optional parameter (path) is the location of the subdirectory containing the file. Discussion of this parameter will be postponed until Chapter 6, when fixed disk systems that typically use subdirectories are discussed in detail.

DOS requires that a **filename** be at least one character in length, but it can be as long as eight characters. Filenames can be made up of numeric digits, alphabetic letters, and certain special characters. You should avoid using any of the special characters, except for possibly the hyphen (-), which is used to make filenames more readable.

The final parameter is an optional **extension**. The extension is comprised of the same set of characters that are valid for filenames, but is limited to three characters. If an extension is used, it must be preceded by a period. Example: **A:JONES86.DOC**

The intended purpose of a filename extension is to indicate the category of each file. Using filename extensions is highly recommended to aid in keeping track of your files. Extensions can be very beneficial when used in conjunction with the global characters discussed in the next section.

When creating filenames, you should always use meaningful titles to further classify the type of data contained in each file. You can code a great deal of information into your filenames. For example, a set of memos on the new bottling plant could be named BOTTLE1.DOC, BOTTLE2.DOC, etc. Or, if the memo date was critical, the set could be named BOTmm-dd.DOC, where the mm represented the month created and the dd the day. Later you will see how global characters could be used to selectively copy only the desired category of files. When sorted file directories are displayed, the memos would appear listed together in chronological sequence. As the number of your saved files grows, the benefits of care and foresight in creating filenames may become more obvious to you.

When you assign file extensions, you should abide by the standard extensions already established by DOS and common application programs. Some fairly standard extensions are described in Figure 2-3.

The $$$ extension is normally used by various application programs to identify temporary work files that the program intends to delete prior to completion. If you see any of these files on a directory listing, it is an indication that a program terminated abnormally, which could be due to such things as a power failure or a user-initiated break.

$$$ - scratch or temporary file (pipeline in DOS).
BAK - backup file.
BAS - BASIC program file (needs compiling first).
BAT - executable batch file (file of DOS commands).
COM - executable command file (machine language), type in the filename and press the Return key.
DAT - data file (listable via the TYPE command).
DBF - dBaseIII file.
DEF - program definition or setup file.
DOC - documentation file, similar to DAT.
EXE - executable file, similar to COM file, but must be allocated to a specific memory location.
MSG - message file, similar to DAT and DOC.
PRN - printer file (can be modified prior to printing).
SYS - operating system file (like a device driver).
TXT - text file, similar to DAT, DOC and MSG.
WKS - Lotus 1-2-3 worksheet file.

Figure 2-3 Standard Filename Extensions

Global Characters

Global characters have been referred to as **wildcard characters** because, like jokers in a card game, they can be used to represent different characters in DOS commands. The two global characters used by DOS are the asterisk (*), representing a group of characters, and the question mark (?), representing only a single character.

Perhaps the best way to understand the use of global characters is by example. If you wished to display a directory listing of all of the files on Drive A that begin with the characters LTR and that have an extension of DOC, you could enter the following directory (DIR) command: **DIR A:LTR*.DOC**

In this example, the asterisk will substitute for any group of characters, such that filenames of LTRSMITH.DOC, LTR4.DOC, and LTRBILL3.DOC would all qualify to be displayed in the directory.

If you wished to display all of the files on Drive A that only contained a single character following LTR and contained any filename extension, you could enter: **DIR A:LTR?.***

30 INTRODUCTION TO DOS

In this example, the filenames of LTR1.DOC, LTR2, and LTRX.TXT would be displayed in the directory. Global characters can also be used with optional filename extensions (for example, DIR A:TEXT.*).

Try some examples using your DOS disk. Enter the following three commands at the A system prompt:

      DIR (to list all files on Drive A)
DIR A:*.EXE (lists just those with an EXE extension)
 DIR A:S*.* (lists just those that begin with an "S")

Figure 2-4 shows you what the display screen might look like after executing the last two commands, assuming Drive A contained PC-DOS Version 3.1.

```
A>DIR A:*.EXE

   Volume in drive A is DOS DISK
   Directory of  A:\

ATTRIB    EXE    15091   3-07-85   1:43p
FIND      EXE     6403   3-07-85   1:43p
JOIN      EXE    15971   3-07-85   1:43p
SHARE     EXE     8304   3-07-85   1:43p
SORT      EXE     1664   3-07-85   1:43p
SUBST     EXE    16611   3-07-85   1:43p
       6 File(s)      44032 bytes free

A>DIR A:S*.*

   Volume in drive A is DOS DISK
   Directory of  A:\

SELECT    COM     2084   3-07-85   1:43p
SHARE     EXE     8304   3-07-85   1:43p
SORT      EXE     1664   3-07-85   1:43p
SUBST     EXE    16611   3-07-85   1:43p
SYS       COM     3727   3-07-85   1:43p
       5 File(s)      44032 bytes free
```

Figure 2-4 Data displayed on Monitor

The DOS Directory Listing

When you get a directory listing on your screen, more than just the filenames will be displayed. The file size, in bytes, as well as a "date stamp" is also displayed for each file. The date stamp is the date and time that each file was last written to the disk. As the number of files saved becomes large, the need to have the correct date stamp becomes even more important. This is why it is important to correctly enter the date and time each time DOS is booted. Figure 2-5 shows you a directory listing of a DOS disk (in this case PC-DOS Version 3.1) for a typical IBM clone.

```
Volume in drive A has no label
Directory of  A:\
COMMAND  COM    23210    3-07-85   1:43p
ANSI     SYS     1651    3-07-85   1:43p
ASSIGN   COM     1509    3-07-85   1:43p
ATTRIB   EXE    15091    3-07-85   1:43p
BACKUP   COM     5577    3-07-85   1:43p
BASIC    COM    17792    3-07-85   1:43p
BASICA   COM    27520    3-07-85   1:43p
CHKDSK   COM     9435    3-07-85   1:43p
COMP     COM     3664    3-07-85   1:43p
DISKCOMP COM     4073    3-07-85   1:43p
DISKCOPY COM     4329    3-07-85   1:43p
EDLIN    COM     7261    3-07-85   1:43p
FDISK    COM     8173    3-07-85   1:43p
FIND     EXE     6403    3-07-85   1:43p
FORMAT   COM     9398    3-07-85   1:43p
GRAFTABL COM     1169    3-07-85   1:43p
GRAPHICS COM     3111    3-07-85   1:43p
JOIN     EXE    15971    3-07-85   1:43p
LABEL    COM     1826    3-07-85   1:43p
MODE     COM     5295    3-07-85   1:43p
PRINT    COM     8291    3-07-85   1:43p
RECOVER  COM     4050    3-07-85   1:43p
RESTORE  COM     5410    3-07-85   1:43p
SELECT   COM     2084    3-07-85   1:43p
SHARE    EXE     8304    3-07-85   1:43p
SORT     EXE     1664    3-07-85   1:43p
SUBST    EXE    16611    3-07-85   1:43p
TREE     COM     2831    3-07-85   1:43p
VDISK    SYS     3307    3-07-85   1:43p
  36 file(s)    77,420 bytes free
```

Figure 2-5 PC-DOS Disk Directory

The directory can be displayed in three general ways. One way is to list all the files with all the information, one after another, until all files have been displayed. To produce this display, simply enter the **DIR command** at the system prompt, a directory of and all filenames on the default drive will be displayed. However, many times disks contain more files than can be displayed on the screen without scrolling. To get a directory listing of filenames a "screenful" at a time, enter **DIR /P**. The "P" option tells DOS to display only a page at a time. The "/" identifies a command option to DOS. After displaying a page of filenames, it will ask you to press any key to see additional filenames displayed. Another way the directory can be displayed is with the "W" option. This option is helpful if you do not need to have the file size and date stamp displayed, because it will display only the filenames, listing them five to a line, in "wide" format. To use this option, enter **DIR /W**. Figure 2-6 shows you what the "wide" format looks like.

```
A>dir /w

   Volume in drive A is DOS DISK
   Directory of  A:\

COMMAND  COM      ANSI     SYS      ASSIGN   COM      ATTRIB   EXE      BACKUP   COM
BASIC    COM      BASICA   COM      CHKDSK   COM      COMP     COM      DISKCOMP COM
DISKCOPY COM      EDLIN    COM      FDISK    COM      FIND     EXE      FORMAT   COM
GRAFTABL COM      GRAPHICS COM      JOIN     EXE      KEYBFR   COM      KEYBGR   COM
KEYBIT   COM      KEYBSP   COM      KEYBUK   COM      LABEL    COM      MODE     COM
MORE     COM      PRINT    COM      RECOVER  COM      RESTORE  COM      SELECT   COM
SHARE    EXE      SORT     EXE      SUBST    EXE      SYS      COM      TREE     COM
VDISK    SYS      DEBUG    COM      CONFIG   SYS
       38 File(s)     44032 bytes free

A>
```

Figure 2-6 Example of DIR with "Wide" Option

Internal vs. External Commands

DOS commands are of two general types, internal and external. **Internal commands**, included with the portion of DOS that is loaded into RAM when the system is booted, are available after the boot process loads the COMMAND.COM file from the system disk. Because it is much faster to access commands from RAM, the designers of the operating system have made the more commonly used commands internal. Some of the more commonly used internal commands include DIR, TYPE, and COPY.

Because the full set of DOS commands is too extensive to be completely loaded into RAM, a substantial number of commands, called **external commands**, reside on the DOS disk. External commands include CHKDSK, FORMAT, and SORT. Later on you will see how you can create your own external commands, referred to as batch files.

DOS automatically translates all commands to upper case characters, so you can enter DOS commands using either upper case or lower case letters. Futhermore, commands can be entered using a combination of both types. For example, the commands Dir, dir, and DIR are treated the same way by DOS. To help you remember this option, our text examples will consistently make use of both upper and lower case letters.

DOS Versions

Figures in this chapter refer specifically to Version 3.x of PC-DOS, where x refers to any one of the major modification sub-levels. Major releases of DOS generally accompany a major change or improvement in hardware design. The first version (DOS 1.x) was somewhat limited and is now considered quite obsolete. DOS 2.x added fixed disk capability, a necessity for most business applications. DOS 3.x added networking capability, better file management commands, and the ability to use the new 3 1/2 inch disks. The next version of PC-DOS, OS/2, will exploit the power of the new high-speed chips (Intel 80286/80386), concurrency (the running of multiple programs at the same time), and more RAM (currently limited to 640K). If you have a 2.x version of PC-DOS, it may be worth the $80 or so, and some restoring of files, to upgrade to the latest 3.x version. The 3.x versions contain the following useful additions:

      ATTRIB - a command that allows you to protect a file by making it a "read-only" file.
      LABEL - a command that allows you to add, change, or delete a disk's volume label (an internal label).
      VDISK.SYS - a device driver that enables you to use part of RAM as a very fast, disk drive. This is called RAMDRIVE.SYS in MS-DOS.

FORMATTING DISKS WITH DOS

In order for files to be saved on disk, the disk must be properly prepared to accept the data to be saved. When you purchase a new blank disk, it is basically a "generic" disk that can be used with many different microcomputers, including a variety of different operating systems. Therefore, each blank disk (floppy or fixed) must be customized according to the requirements of DOS. This customizing process is called **formatting** and includes the following internal operations:

1. Create addressable areas of the disk, made up of clusters, where data can be safely stored. Since each disk drive and operating system have their own addressing scheme, this activity is mandatory prior to saving files. With DOS 2.x and later versions, each of the 40 tracks on one side of a floppy disk is divided into 9 sectors, a total of 360 sectors (40 x 9 = 360). Each sector is designed to hold 512 bytes of data. A cluster is a corresponding track and sector on both sides of a disk. A computer's address for storing data is a beginning cluster number.

2. Check every recording spot on the new disk for damage and determine which clusters, if any, are not acceptable for storing data.

3. Create a directory area and a File Allocation Table (FAT) on the disk that can be used by DOS to keep track of the files saved. The addresses of any unacceptable disk clusters and the addresses of all files saved are recorded in the FAT.

The **FORMAT command** is used to prepare a disk for use by DOS. When you format a disk, the system will display the status of your disk, including the number of bytes in any bad sectors (clusters) it finds. Here is an example of the information displayed after the command FORMAT was entered and the disk being formatted had some unacceptable sectors:

```
160256  bytes total disk space
  8192  bytes in bad sectors
152064  bytes available on disk
```

The FORMAT command offers several helpful options. The first, "system" or "S" option tells DOS to format the disk and include the DOS boot programs on the disk. When DOS formats a disk with the "S" option, it actually writes three files on the disk. Two of these are hidden, which means you cannot see them when you display a directory of that disk. The third file, which is not hidden, is the COMMAND.COM file that contains all of the internal DOS commands. To use the "S" option, to create "bootable" disks, enter FORMAT /S.

Another helpful option of the FORMAT command is the "V" option, which allows you to name your disk, referred to as a volume label or "internal" file label. This option is especially helpful when working with numerous disks, because it helps you keep track of your files. The "V" option allows you to create a name for each disk that can be viewed on the screen without having to remove the disk from the drive, a requirement with "external" labels. To use the "V" option, enter **FORMAT /V**. To use it with the "system" option, enter **FORMAT /S/V** or **FORMAT /V/S**.

Beginning with version 3.2 of DOS, the FORMAT command will no longer assume you want to format the default drive if you enter the command without any parameters. This precaution will keep you from attempting to reformat your DOS disk accidentally.

Review Questions for Chapter 2

1. What are the main purposes of an operating system?
2. What is meant by the term "booting the system"?
3. What are the hidden files on a DOS disk?
4. Why is it important to write on both sides of a floppy disk before moving to another track?
5. Why is it important to boot your system with the correct date and time?
6. What is the function of the File Allocation Table?
7. What is the difference between a warm boot and a cold boot?
8. How do you activate a warm boot?
9. What is the purpose of the COMMAND.COM file?
10. What is the purpose of the AUTOEXEC.BAT file?
11. How can you change the system date once the system is booted?
12. How would you enter a time of 2:35pm when prompted to do so.
13. What does the command "DIR B:/W" do when executed?
14. What is the purpose of the FORMAT command?

15. What do the standard device names CON and PRN represent?
16. What is a filename extension and how is it identified by DOS?
17. What kind of file would likely have an extension of ".$$$"?
18. What are some common extensions for listable files?
19. What are some common extensions for executable files?
20. Why would you ever want to use the /S option with FORMAT?

DOS Lab Exercise #1

PLEASE NOTE:

This exercise assumes that the system is already turned on from a prior class demonstration. If not, boot the system according to what you learned in this chapter. All of these exercises were developed for computers with two floppy disk drives. Drive A will hold DOS and Drive B will hold your working data disk.

If you are working with a fixed disk system with only one floppy disk, the following modifications must be made to your exercises:

- The DOS commands should already be loaded to your fixed disk (C:), so you should turn on the power to the CPU without having any disk in the floppy drive. Change any reference to Drive A in the exercises to Drive C.
- Floppy drive (A:) will be used to hold your working data disk. Therefore, change any reference to Drive B in the exercises to Drive A.

1. **Warm Boot:**
    - With the DOS disk in Drive A, use **Control-Alt-Del** to boot the system.
    - Enter the date in mm-dd-yy format (i.e., 9-15-87)
    - Enter the time in hh:mm format (i.e., 13:07)
    - Don't forget to press the Enter key (or Return) to cause the computer to act upon your data.

2. **Format a data disk to contain the DOS system files:**
    - Enter FORMAT b:/s/v
    - Insert a blank disk in Drive B and press Enter
    - Enter your name (up to 11 characters) when prompted to do so by the system
    - Enter "n" when prompted to format another disk.

Figure 2-7 shows you what the screen should look like when you finish formatting your blank disk.

```
A>FORMAT B:/s/v
Insert new diskette for drive B:
and strike ENTER when ready

Formatting...Format complete
System transferred

Volume label (11 characters, ENTER for none)? Data Disk

    362496 bytes total disk space
     62464 bytes used by system
    300032 bytes available on disk

Format another (Y/N)?n
A>
```

Figure 2-7 Screen Display

3. **Create a file from the keyboard:**
   - Enter COPY CON B:READ.ME (or copy con b:read.me)
   - Then, on the lines that follow, enter this text, pressing the Enter key at the end of each line:

When entering DOS commands, the commands and parameters must be separated by delimiters. Delimiters are normally either a space, a comma, or a semicolon. They can be used interchangeably within any command (i.e., COPY A:oldfile,B:).

   - When done entering lines of text, press the special function key **F6** (to tell DOS you are done with the copy operation) and press Enter. The text you just keyed will then be stored on the disk in Drive B with the filename of READ.ME.

Figure 2-8 shows you the screen after you have completed the COPY CON command.

```
A>COPY CON B:READ.ME
When entering DOS commands, the commands and parameters
must be separated by delimiters.  Delimiters are normally
either a space, a comma, or a semicolon.  They can be used
interchangeably within any command (ie. COPY A:oldfile,B:)
^Z
        1 File(s) copied

A>
```

Figure 2-8 Screen Display

4. **Display a disk file on the monitor:**
   - Enter **DIR B:** (to see if your file was stored OK). This will give you a listing of your file plus the COMMAND.COM file placed there during formatting.
   - Now enter **TYPE B:READ.ME** to see a display of your text file on the monitor.

Figure 2-9 shows you what the screen should look like when you finish this portion of the exercise.

```
A>dir b:

 Volume in drive B is DATA DISK
 Directory of  B:\

COMMAND  COM     23210   3-07-85   1:43p
READ     ME        236   9-25-87   2:38p
        2 File(s)    299008 bytes free

A>type b:read.me
When entering DOS commands, the commands and parameters
must be separated by delimiters.  Delimiters are normally
either a space, a comma, or a semicolon.  They can be used
interchangeably within any command (ie. COPY A:oldfile,B:)
A>
```

Figure 2-9 Display Screen

5. **COPY a file to a disk:**
   - Enter **COPY B:READ.ME B:READ.BAK** This will create a duplicate copy of your file, but with a different filename (i.e., the extension will be BAK rather than ME).
   - Now enter **DIR B:** (to get a directory listing of B). You should have three files listed on your data disk: COMMAND.COM, READ.ME, and READ.BAK.

   Figure 2-10 shows the display screen at this point.

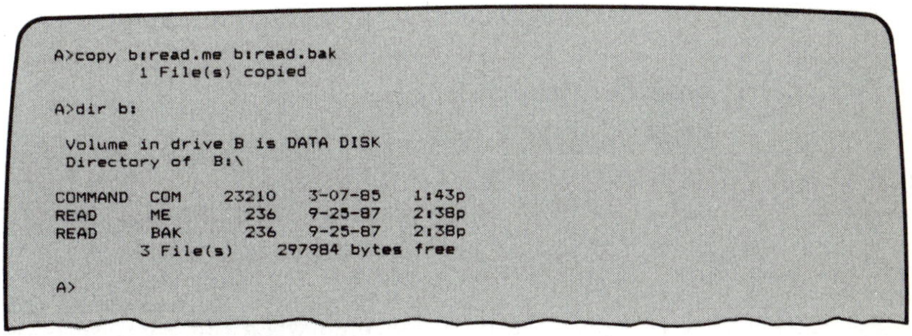

   ```
   A>copy b:read.me b:read.bak
           1 File(s) copied

   A>dir b:

    Volume in drive B is DATA DISK
    Directory of  B:\

   COMMAND  COM   23210   3-07-85   1:43p
   READ     ME      236   9-25-87   2:38p
   READ     BAK     236   9-25-87   2:38p
           3 File(s)    297984 bytes free

   A>
   ```

   Figure 2-10 Screen Display

6. **DELete a file from a disk:**
   - Enter **DEL B:READ.BAK**
   - Now, enter **DIR B:** (to verify the file was deleted).

   Your screen should contain the data similar to that shown in Figure 2-11.

```
A>del b:read.me

A>dir b:

 Volume in drive B is DATA DISK
 Directory of  B:\

COMMAND  COM    23210   3-07-85   1:43p
READ     BAK      236   9-25-87   2:38p
    2 File(s)      299008 bytes free

A>
```

Figure 2-11 Screen display

7. **Change the default disk drive:**
   - Enter B:(to switch default to Drive B)
   - Now, enter DIR(to get a directory of the default disk, Drive B).
   - Enter DIR A:/W(to get a wide listing of Drive A).
   - Enter A:(to place the default drive back to Drive A.)

Figure 2-12 shows the display screen when this exercise is over. Some of data you may still have on your screen is shown in this figure. Don't be concerned if several of the top lines have scrolled off the top of your screen.

```
A>B:

B>dir

 Volume in drive B is DATA DISK
 Directory of  B:\

COMMAND  COM    23210   3-07-85   1:43p
READ     BAK      236   9-25-87   2:38p
        2 File(s)    299008 bytes free

B>dir a:/w

 Volume in drive A is DOS DISK
 Directory of  A:\

COMMAND  COM   ANSI     SYS   ASSIGN   COM   ATTRIB   EXE   BACKUP   COM
BASIC    COM   BASICA   COM   CHKDSK   COM   COMP     COM   DISKCOMP COM
DISKCOPY COM   EDLIN    COM   FDISK    COM   FIND     EXE   FORMAT   COM
GRAFTABL COM   GRAPICS  COM   JOIN     EXE   KEYBFR   COM   KEYBGR   COM
KEYBIT   COM   KEYBSP   COM   KEYBUK   COM   LABEL    COM   MODE     COM
MORE     COM   PRINT    COM   RECOVER  COM   RESTORE  COM   SELECT   COM
SHARE    EXE   SORT     EXE   SUBST    EXE   SYS      COM   TREE     COM
VDISK    SYS   DEBUG    COM   CONFIG   SYS
       38 File(s)    44032 bytes free

B>A:

A>
```

Figure 2-12 Screen Display

This completes the first lab exercise. Remove your floppy disks and turn off the computer. Thank you!

Chapter 3

INTERNAL FLOPPY DISK COMMANDS

DOS INTERNAL COMMANDS
    BREAK (Control Break) Command
    CLS (Clear Screen) Command
    COPY Command
    DATE Command
    DEL (Delete) Command
    DIR (Directory) Command
    PROMPT Command
    RENAME Command
    TIME Command
    TYPE Command
    VER (Version) Command
    VERIFY Command
    VOL (Volume Label) Command

Chapter 3

INTERNAL FLOPPY DISK COMMANDS

To make it easier to remember which of the commands are internal and which are external, the DOS commands covered in this chapter are all internal. External floppy disk commands are covered in Chapter 4.

This chapter covers 13 internal DOS commands that can be used with floppy disk systems. Many of these commands are also applicable to fixed disk systems, but do not require fixed disks. More advanced DOS commands, those used primarily with fixed disk systems, will be covered in later chapters.

Our discussion of each command includes:

1. the general format of the command,
2. an explanation of the command parameters,
3. helpful options when using the command, and
4. some examples of usage.

In addition to the command name itself, DOS commands can contain various **parameters** to indicate the target of the command, as well as **options** to indicate how the command is be executed. Command parameters and options that apply primarily to fixed disk systems will be bypassed for now.

If the format of a command has a parameter or option enclosed in **brackets** ([ ]), that part of the command is not always required. Do not include the brackets as part of the command when entering it. Command options are always preceded by a **slash** (/). We have intentionally omitted command options that are seldom used.

A **delimiter** is a special character used to define the end of a word or specific portion of DOS commands. Commands and associated parameters must be separated by a delimiter. DOS uses a variety of delimiters, including a space, a comma, a semicolon, an equal sign, or the tab key. The examples in this text will use only the space as a delimiter. As mentioned in Chapter 2, you can enter commands using any combination of upper- or lower-case characters.

The execution of commands can be stopped prior to normal completion in a variety of ways. You can abort DOS commands when they are running by entering **Ctrl-C** (or Ctrl-Break). When commands display a large amount of output on the screen, **Ctrl-S** will temporarily suspend the display. The pressing of any key will continue the display process. When software instructions direct you to "press any key ...", this normally refers to any alpha (A-Z), numeric (0-9), or the space bar. It does not refer to any of the special or control keys.

A command you enter may be rejected by DOS, spurring an error message such as **Bad Command or File Name**. You will see this message if the command entered was not spelled correctly, or if a filename entered was not on the disk specified. If this error message appears, simply retype the command correctly.

If you are attempting to read a disk and no disk is in the designated drive, the drive latch is open, or an unformatted disk is placed in the drive, you will get the following two-line error message:

**Disk error reading Drive __
Abort, Retry, Ignore?**

If you get this message, correct the problem and enter an "R" to retry. (You can also enter an "A" to abort the command or an "I" to ignore the error condition.) Do not change disks before responding with Abort, Retry, or Ignore.

Because the space between the read/write heads and the surface of the disks is incredibly small, any movement of the disk drive when the disk is operating can be very destructive. When previously recorded data has been damaged, you will see the following message displayed when you attempt to access the damaged data:

General Failure reading Drive __
Abort, Retry, or Ignore?

For a more complete description of commands and error messages, consult the DOS manual.

DOS INTERNAL COMMANDS

All of the internal commands are contained in the COMMAND.COM file that is loaded to main memory when DOS is booted. Therefore, you do not need to have the system disk in a disk drive when attempting to execute internal commands. The internal commands, covered alphabetically in this chapter, include:

1. **BREAK** - turn the system break mode on or off
2. **CLS** (Clear Screen) - clear the screen of all data
3. **COPY** - make a copy of a disk file
4. **DATE** - display and/or change the system date
5. **DEL** (Delete) - delete a file from disk
6. **DIR** (Directory) - display filenames from a disk
7. **PROMPT** - change the system prompt
8. **RENAME** - change the name of an existing file
9. **TIME** - display and/or change the system time
10. **TYPE** - display the contents of a listable disk file
11. **VER** (Version) - display the version number of DOS
12. **VERIFY** - turn the verify mode on or off
13. **VOL** (Volume) - display a disk volume label

BREAK (Control Break) Command

Format: BREAK [ON|OFF]

The **BREAK command** sets a switch in DOS that controls when the system should check for Ctrl-Break (or Ctrl-C) from the keyboard. With Break set off (the default setting), DOS will only check for Ctrl-Break during input/output operations to the keyboard, screen or printer. To direct DOS to additionally check for Ctrl-Break during disk I/O operations, you must set Break on by executing the BREAK command. This option is useful when you run programs that are difficult to stop. If you enter BREAK with no parameters, the current status of Break is displayed on the screen. This command is often included in the CONFIG.SYS file (covered in Chapter 7).

Examples of usage:

    A> **Break on**   (direct DOS to "break-out" of a program as soon as Ctrl-Break is pressed)
    A> **BREAK OFF** (direct DOS to only check for Ctrl-Break during input/output operations)
    A> **break** (display the current status of Break)

CLS (Clear Screen) Command

Format: **CLS**

The **CLS command** clears the monitor (display screen) to all blanks.

COPY Command

Format: **COPY [d:]filename[.ext] [d:][filename[.ext]] [/V]**, where the first filename is the source file and the second (optional) filename is the target file (the new file being created).

The **COPY command** lets you make copies of disk files to a previously formatted disk. It facilitates making backup or working copies of files without destroying existing files. (Note: Any files on the target disk with the same name as the target file will be replaced by the contents of the source file after the COPY command has executed.)

    If you omit the disk device designator (d:), DOS will substitute the default device. If you omit the optional target filename, the system will use the same filename as the source file. Be sure to include appropriate filename extensions. To verify that sectors written on the target disk were recorded properly, use the /V option. This option will slow down the copy process, but may be worthwhile if you are experiencing disk problems. For example:

    COPY   A:MYFILE.TXT   B:MYFILE.BAK /V

Concatenation, the combining of files, can be performed with the copy command. Use COPY with the plus (+) symbol between multiple source filenames to combine two or more source files into a single, new target file. For example:

COPY   A:FILEA.DOC+A:FILEB.DOC   B:NEWFILE.DOC

Files combined with the COPY command may have two **end of file** (or EOF) marks, displayed as Ctrl-Z. To make the file more useful, you can edit the file with the DOS line editor (EDLIN, covered in Chapter 5), removing the EOF mark in middle of the target file.

You can copy a group of files with a single command by using global characters with the COPY command in filenames and filename extensions. For example:

COPY   A:*.DOC   B:

If you specify the source file as CON (for CONsole keyboard), the target file will contain characters entered from the keyboard. Type characters as you would from a typewriter, pressing the Enter key at the end of each line. To stop recording characters, press the **F6** function key <F6> followed by the Enter key. For example:

COPY   CON   A:KBFILE.TXT (followed by lines of text and <F6>)

COPY CON can easily be used to type a "quick and dirty" two- or three-line file of text, but it is not appropriate for larger files. DOS provides EDLIN (see Chapter 5) for larger text files.

Examples of usage:

- A> **COPY   *.*   B:** (copies all files on the default disk, Drive A, to the disk in Drive B, without renaming files)
- A> **copy   B: *.DOC** (copies all files on Drive B with an extension of "doc" to the default disk without renaming files)
- A> **Copy   filea.doc   b:filea.bak** (copies FILEA.DOC on Drive A to Drive B, renaming it FILEA.BAK)
- A> **copy   con   B:read.me** (creates a file on Drive B named READ.ME consisting of data entered from console)

A> **copy a.txt + b.txt   c.txt** (creates a new file, c.txt, as a combination of a.txt and b.txt)
A> **copy filea.doc   B:/V** (copies filea.doc on Drive A to Drive B and directs DOS to verify the copy)
A> **copy FILEA.DOC   PRN** (copies an ASCII file to the printer)
A> **copy con   prn** (lets you to use your keyboard like a typewriter)

DATE Command

Format: DATE [mm-dd-yy]

The **DATE command** allows you to change the system date. If you specify a new date (i.e., 11-15-87) when you enter the command, it will be changed immediately. If you omit this optional parameter, the system will display the current date and prompt you to enter a new date. Press the Enter key if you do not wish to change it. If you enter an invalid date, you will be prompted to re-enter a correct date.

Examples of usage:

A> **DATE   3/4/87** (changes the system date to March 4, 1987)
A> **date   03-04-87** (changes the system date to March 4, 1987)
A> **Date** (displays the current date and prompts you to change it)

DEL (Delete) Command

Format: DEL [d:]filename[.ext]

The **DEL command** deletes the specified disk file. If the drive designator is not specified, the default drive is assumed. You can use global characters (* and ?) in the filename and extension, but do so with caution, as multiple files can quickly be deleted with a single command. If you use *.* to specify the file, all files on the designated disk will be deleted. When you attempt to delete all files on a disk, the DELETE command gives you some measure of protection against eliminating files by mistake: it pauses to ask you if you are sure. You will not be allowed to delete "read-only" files without first changing the status with the ATTRIB command which is discussed in Chapter 4.

The term "delete" may be a little misleading, since files are not physically deleted from a disk file. The DEL command merely causes the file's entry on the disk's directory to be physically removed, thereby allowing other data to eventually be written over the "deleted" file.

Since the **ERASE** command is identical to the DEL command, ERASE is not specifically covered in this text. With DOS, ERASE is treated as just another spelling of DEL.

Examples of usage:

    A> **DEL**   **a:Memo.txt** (deletes file Memo.txt from drive A)
    A> **DEL**   **memo.txt** (deletes file MEMO.TXT from the default drive)
    A> **del**   ***.txt** (deletes all files on the default drive with a filename extension of .txt)

DIR (Directory) Command

Format: **DIR**   **[d:] [filename[.ext]] [/P] [/W]**

The **DIR command** displays a directory, or listing, of the files on a specified disk. The information provided in the listing includes the volume identification, the names of each file, the size in bytes of each file, the date and time each file was last written to, and the amount of free space left on the disk. If you do not designate a disk drive, DOS will use the default drive. If you specify a filename, then the directory will be limited to only that name. Since the filename can contain global characters, the directory can be limited to a specific group of files.

Use the **/P** option to cause the computer to "pause" during display of the directory when the screen is full. It will continue displaying again after you press any key to signal you are ready. Figure 3-1 shows what the screen might look like using the **pause option**.

```
dir a:/p

Volume in drive A is DOS DISK
Directory of  A:\

COMMAND   COM     23210   3-07-85   1:43p
ANSI      SYS      1651   3-07-85   1:43p
ASSIGN    COM      1509   3-07-85   1:43p
ATTRIB    EXE     15091   3-07-85   1:43p
BACKUP    COM      5577   3-07-85   1:43p
BASIC     COM     17792   3-07-85   1:43p
BASICA    COM     27520   3-07-85   1:43p
CHKDSK    COM      9435   3-07-85   1:43p
COMP      COM      3664   3-07-85   1:43p
DISKCOMP  COM      4073   3-07-85   1:43p
DISKCOPY  COM      4329   3-07-85   1:43p
EDLIN     COM      7261   3-07-85   1:43p
FDISK     COM      8173   3-07-85   1:43p
FIND      EXE      6403   3-07-85   1:43p
FORMAT    COM      9398   3-07-85   1:43p
GRAFTABL  COM      1169   3-07-85   1:43p
GRAPHICS  COM      3111   3-07-85   1:43p
JOIN      EXE     15971   3-07-85   1:43p
KEYBFR    COM      2473   4-12-85   4:22p
KEYBGR    COM      2418   4-12-85   4:23p
KEYBIT    COM      2361   4-12-85   4:25p
KEYBSP    COM      2451   4-12-85   4:24p
KEYBUK    COM      2348   4-12-85   4:26p
Strike a key when ready . . .
```

Figure 3-1 Screen Display of DIR with /P Option

Use the **/W** option to display the directory in **wide format,** in which only the filenames are displayed across the screen, five files on a line. You can use the /W option to save display time and space.

Subdirectory names (to be covered later) are also displayed on the directory, and are clearly identified with <DIR> in the file size field. Entries for the hidden system files are never listed, even when present.

Examples of usage:

    A> **Dir** (display a directory of all files on the default disk drive)
    A> **DIR   B:** (display a directory of all files in Drive B)
    A> **dir   a:dog*.*** (display directory of Drive A, of only those files with filenames that begin with "dog")
    A> **Dir   b:/p** (display the Drive B directory, pausing after the screen fills up)
    A> **dir   /w** (display filenames from the default drive in "wide" format)

A> **DIR /w/P** (display filenames from the default disk in "wide" format, pausing after each screen)

PROMPT Command

Format: **PROMPT [text]**, where text is a variable-length string of characters. Text may contain special strings in the form of $c, where c represents one of the following:

t - the system time
d - the system date
n - the default drive
g - the > character
_ - the "new line" command (use underline key to skip a line)
p - display the current directory (Chapter 6)
e - send an ESCape character (Chapter 7)

The **PROMPT command** allows you to change the system prompt from the default (A>) to whatever you want to make it. Placing a PROMPT command in your AUTOEXEC.BAT file ensures that your "customized" prompt appears automatically each time you boot DOS. If you enter PROMPT with no text, the system will revert back to the default prompt. For more information on PROMPT, consult the DOS manual. Figure 3-2 shows the effect on the screen of executing the following four commands.

Examples of usage:

A> **PROMPT Command?** (changes the system prompt from "A>" to "Command?")
A> **prompt DATE = $d** (changes the system prompt to display "DATE =", followed by the system date)
A> **prompt Hi Fred $_$n$g** (displays "Hi Fred" on the first system prompt line followed by "A>")
A> **PROMPT** (return to the normal system prompt)

```
A>prompt Command?

Command?prompt DATE = $d

DATE = Sat 10-03-1987prompt Hi Fred $_$n$g
Hi Fred
A>prompt
A>
```

Figure 3-2 Display of Changing Prompts

RENAME Command

Format: **RENAME [d:]filename[.ext] filename[.ext]**

The **RENAME command** changes the name of the file specified in the first parameter to the filename and extension given in the second parameter. A drive designator is not required in the second parameter and will be rejected if entered. RENAME gives you an easy way to make disguised copies of important files.

Examples of usage:

- A> **RENAME   b:ltr1.doc   ltr1.bak** (renames ltr1.doc on Drive B to ltr1.bak)
- A> **rename   Ltr1.doc   ltr1.bak** (renames ltr1.doc on Drive A to ltr1.bak)
- A> **Rename   ltr1.doc   *.bak**   (renames ltr1.doc on Drive A to ltr1.bak --- Note: use of global characters can save keystrokes)

TIME Command

Format: **TIME [hh:mm[:ss]]**

The **TIME command** allows you to change the system time. It is important to keep the correct date and time on the system because it is recorded in the directory information of each file you save. If you omit the optional parameters, the current system time will be displayed and you will be prompted to change it. To leave the time as is, just press the Enter key. If you enter an invalid time, the system will prompt you to re-enter a new time.

Examples of usage:

    A> **TIME 8:30** (changes the system time to 8:30 AM)
    A> **Time 14:15:35** (changes the time to 2:15 PM and 35 seconds)
    A> **time** (displays the current time and prompts you to enter a new time)
    A> **time 11.55.30** (changes the time to 11:55 AM and 30 seconds)

TYPE Command

    Format: **TYPE [d:]filename[.ext]**

The **TYPE command** is used to display the contents of a "listable" file on the standard output device, normally the monitor. It does not alter files. This command should only be used for ASCII text files, not files that end with an extension of .EXE or .COM. Global characters are not allowed. You can use the Print Screen function to display the contents of a file on the printer. You can also redirect the output to another file or to a printer, a topic covered in the next chapter.

Examples of usage:

    A> **TYPE   B:READ.ME** (displays the contents of read.me, stored on Drive B, on the monitor)
    A> **type   read.me** (displays read.me, stored on the default drive, on the monitor)

VER (Version) Command

    Format: **VER**

The **VER command** will display on the screen the DOS version number being used (i.e., **IBM Personal Computer DOS Version 3.10**).

VERIFY Command

Format: **VERIFY [ON|OFF]**

The **VERIFY command** sets the Verify mode in DOS that controls when the system should verify that data it writes on a disk has been correctly recorded. With Verify set off (the default), DOS will not perform a verify operation each time a write operation takes place. To direct DOS to verify each write operation, you must set Verify on with the VERIFY command. Because of the extra time required to perform verification, the system will run in approximately twice the time when writing to a disk. Write verification is not recommended unless you are experiencing problems reading your disks. If you enter VERIFY with no parameters, the current status of Verify will be displayed on the screen. Examples of usage:

A> **VERIFY on** (directs DOS to verify each disk write)
A> **verify off** (sets the Verify mode off)
A> **Verify** (displays the current status of the verify mode)

VOL (Volume Label) Command

Format: **VOL [d:]**

The **VOL command** is used to display the internal disk volume label of the designated drive, so you don't have to physically remove the disk from the drive to identify it. If you do not specify a drive, the default drive is assumed. The volume label can be created with the FORMAT command and changed with the LABEL command. Both of these commands are external commands, covered in the next chapter.

Example of usage:

A> **vol B:** (displays the volume label recorded on the disk in Drive B; i.e., **Volume in drive B has no label**)
A> **VOL** (displays the volume label of Drive A)

Review Questions for Chapter 3

1. What is the function of brackets ([ ]) in this text for describing command formats?
2. What is the function of the slash (/) in this text for describing command formats?
3. What is a delimiter and why is it required?
4. What does the message "Bad Command or File Name" mean?
5. Where are internal commands stored on a permanent basis?
6. When does DOS normally check for a Ctrl-Break (Ctrl-C) entered from the keyboard?
7. What DOS command blanks out the display screen?
8. What is the benefit of using global characters in the COPY command?
9. What command lets you use the keyboard and printer as a typewriter?
10. What command removes the filename from the disk directory, but does not physically remove the file from the disk?
11. What option allows you to get a a directory listing on the screen with filenames displayed in multiple columns?
12. What method is used to get a directory listing of a specific group of files?
13. What command is used to change the system prompt to display the system time?
14. How would you cause the system to display a customized system prompt every time the system was booted?
15. What happens if you include a disk drive designator on both parameters of the RENAME command?
16. What do you have to enter to change the system time to 4am?
17. What type of file is considered "listable" with TYPE?
18. What command is used to verify the DOS version being used?
19. What command is used to verify that disk writing is correct?
20. What command is used to display the internal label on a disk without getting a directory listing?

DOS Lab Exercise #2

1. Boot DOS (Drive A) and insert your data disk in Drive B. Then enter **DIR B:** to refresh your memory of the files on Drive B. You should have two files shown that were previously created in Lab Exercise #1: COMMAND.COM and READ.ME
2. Enter **VERIFY** to see whether or not DOS verifies each "write" with an automatic "verification read." The responding message should indicate that the verify mode is OFF. Test the effect by entering **COPY A:COMMAND.COM B:TEST.1**, and making a note of how long it takes to copy (i.e., 4 seconds). Enter **VERIFY ON** to set on the verify mode. Enter **COPY A:COMMAND.COM B:TEST.2** and see if the copy with the verification takes a substantially longer time (i.e., 7 seconds). Then, enter **VERIFY OFF**.
3. Enter **DIR B:** to get a current directory listing of your data disk. Enter **RENAME B:TEST.2 TEST.3** to change the filename of TEST.2 on your data disk to TEST.3. Enter **DIR B:** to verify the name change. To simplify the commands in this step, you could have first changed the default disk to Drive B.
4. Enter **VOL B:** to see if your data disk has an internal volume label. If you did not use the /V option when you formatted the disk (or have not yet used the LABEL command), your data disk should not contain a volume label.
5. Enter **VER** to see what DOS version you are using (i.e., Ver. 3.2)
6. Enter **DATE** and follow the system prompts to change the current system date. Then, do the same for **TIME**. Typically, you only need to enter hh:mm (i.e., 13:45) for time, ignoring seconds.
7. Create a combined file: **COPY B:READ.ME+B:READ.ME B:TEST.4** This will create a new file (TEST.4 on Drive B) as the sum, or concatenation, of two files on Drive B (READ.ME and READ.ME). Enter **DIR B:** to see if the combined new file is twice the size of READ.ME. In addition, enter **TYPE B:TEST.4** to verify that the text in READ.ME was duplicated correctly. Your display screen should now look something like Figure 3-3.

```
A>dir b:

Volume in drive B is DATA DISK
Directory of  B:\
COMMAND   COM     23210   3-07-85   1:43p
TEST      1       23210   3-07-85   1:43p
READ      ME        236   9-25-87   2:38p
TEST      3       23210   3-07-85   1:43p
TEST      4         473  10-03-87   2:18p
        5 File(s)    250880 bytes free

A>type b:test.4
When entering DOS commands, the commands and parameters
must be separated by delimiters.  Delimiters are normally
either a space, a comma, or a semicolon.  They can be used
interchangeably within any command (ie. COPY A:oldfile,B:)
When entering DOS commands, the commands and parameters
must be separated by delimiters.  Delimiters are normally
either a space, a comma, or a semicolon.  They can be used
interchangeably within any command (ie. COPY A:oldfile,B:)

A>
```

Figure 3-3 Display Screen

8. Enter **BREAK** to check the status of the Ctrl-Break mode. After it displays the status, clear the screen to blank with **CLS**.

This completes lab exercise #2. If time permits, experiment further with the internal commands in Chapter 3. If you are done, remove the disks and turn off the computer.

Chapter 4

EXTERNAL FLOPPY DISK COMMANDS

DOS EXTERNAL COMMANDS
    ATTRIB (Attribute) Command
    CHKDSK (Check Disk) Command
    COMP (Compare Files) Command
    DISKCOMP Command
    DISKCOPY Command
    FIND Command
    FORMAT Command
    LABEL (Volume Label) Command
    RECOVER Command
    SYS (System) Command

Chapter 4

EXTERNAL FLOPPY DISK COMMANDS

DOS EXTERNAL COMMANDS

All external commands are preceded with an *optional* disk drive designator, which the computer needs in order to identify the drive containing the external commands. If the designator is omitted, the system assumes the command will be found on the default drive. The 10 external commands covered in this chapter include:

*1. **ATTRIB** - set the "read-only" status of a disk file
2. **CHKDSK** - provide a status report of a disk
3. **COMP** (Compare Files) - compare contents of two files
4. **DISKCOMP** - compare contents of two disks
5. **DISKCOPY** - make a duplicate copy of a disk
6. **FIND** - locate a file containing a set of characters
7. **FORMAT** - prepare a disk for recording DOS files
*8. **LABEL** - create, change or delete a disk volume label

9. **RECOVER** - recover a file with defective sectors
10. **SYS** (System) - copy system files to a formatted disk

*added to DOS Version 3.x; not available in earlier versions

ATTRIB (Attribute) Command

Format: **[d:]ATTRIB [+R|-R] [d:]filename[.ext]**

The **ATTRIB command** allows you to set or reset the read-only file attribute. If you have important files that you don't want accidentally destroyed by overwriting, you can add a degree of safety by marking them as read-only with ATTRIB. Enter +R to set the read-only status and -R to remove it. Files identified as read-only cannot be altered without resetting their status with the ATTRIB command. You may use global characters with this command. If you enter ATTRIB without the optional set/reset parameter [+R|-R], the system will display the current status of the file specified.

Examples of usage:

A> **ATTRIB +r   b:filea.txt** (set filea.txt on Drive B to read-only)
A> **attrib   -r B:*.txt** (set all files on Drive B with a txt extension so they are *not* read-only)
A> **B:attrib +R   read.me** (set READ.ME on the default drive to read-only, using the system disk in Drive B)
A> **ATTRIB   B:READ.ME** (displays the read-only status of read.me on Drive B)

CHKDSK (Check Disk) Command

Format: **[d:]CHKDSK   [d:][filename[.ext]] [/F] [/V]**

The **CHKDSK command** produces a disk status report for a specified disk. It also lists the memory status of the system. After checking the disk, CHKDSK displays any error messages, followed by a status report. Refer to your DOS manual for a description of any error messages that appear. The following is an example of a CHKDSK status report, where the drive designated was a floppy disk:

Volume DATADISK   Created JUL 15, 1987 11:35
362496	bytes total disk space
23528	bytes in 3 hidden files
311296	bytes in 29 user files
27672	bytes available on disk
655360	bytes total memory
568112	bytes free

The three hidden files in the status report represent the volume label and the PC-DOS system files (IBMBIO.COM and IBMDOS.COM) that are hidden from normal directory lists. The bottom portion of the report represents the memory status for a 640K system.

As we discussed in Chapter 2, new files are written to contiguous clusters whenever an area big enough can be found. The recording of an existing file that has been enlarged is a much different process, however. When the original file space has been rewritten, DOS continues writing to the first unallocated cluster on the disk. It writes in consecutive clusters, skipping over those that are already allocated. Consequently, files can easily become fragmented as they expand over time.

If you specify a filename or filenames, CHKDSK displays the number of noncontiguous areas occupied by the file(s). Global characters can be used for the filename. Thus, you can use *.* to determine the extent of file fragmentation on a disk, and then use the COPY command to rewrite fragmented files to a newly formated disk. This process is recommended to improve access speed by eliminating fragmented files.

Lost allocation clusters are parts of files or complete files that are still recorded in the File Allocation Table (FAT), even though they have been deleted from the directory. This segmenting occurs due to some malfunction, generally during the file save process. You can use the /F option to combine any lost allocation clusters on a disk into a file named FILEn.CHK. This is a good command to use periodically, especially if a disk has experienced numerous problems. Advanced users can also use the /F option to direct DOS to fix any errors that are found in the FAT. When the FAT is corrupted, it cannot accurately track files on disk. Therefore, the /F option could result in some loss of data during the "fix" process.

The /V option allows you to display all files (and their complete pathname covered, which we will discuss in Chapter 6) from a specified drive. This option can be very beneficial with fixed disk systems.

Examples of usage:

> A> **CHKDSK** (display a status report for the default drive)
> A> **chkdsk /f** (display a status report for Drive A and fix any errors found in the FAT)
> A> **b:chkdsk a:*.*** (display a status report for Drive A and list any fragmented files, locate CHKDSK command on Drive B)
> A> **chkdsk B:read.me** (display a status report for Drive B and display the number of non-contiguous areas contained in READ.ME)

COMP (Compare Files) Command
FC (File Compare) Command in MS-DOS

Format: **[d:]COMP [d:][filename[.ext]] [d:][filename[.ext]]**

The **COMP command** (**FC command** in MS-DOS) compares the contents of the first file specified to the contents of the second file. You can use this command to compare two supposedly identical files. When the files are not identical, DOS displays an error message for each location that does not match. After ten mismatches, the operation is cancelled by DOS. Obviously, files must be of the same length to be compared. Global characters can be used, allowing for multiple sets of files to be compared. If you do not include any filenames, the system will prompt you to enter them.

Examples of usage:

> A> **B:COMP** (execute the COMP command from Drive B, directing the system to prompt you for the files - this way of execution gives you time to replace the system disk with another disk, if required)
> A> **comp filea.doc filea.bak** (compare the two files specified to see if they are identical)
> A> **Comp A:*.* b:** (compare all identically named files on the two Drives specified)

DISKCOMP Command

Format: **[d:]DISKCOMP [d:[d:]]**

The **DISKCOMP command** compares the contents of the two drives specified. It is only used to compare two entire floppy disks, but not fixed disks. It could be a good command to use if you were making numerous copies of a disk and wanted to verify they were all identical. If you specify only one drive, Diskcomp uses the default drive as the target drive.

DISKCOPY Command

Format: **[d:]DISKCOPY [d:[d:]]**

The **DISKCOPY command** copies the entire contents of one floppy disk to another. It does not require that the target disk be formatted. For that reason, it is *not recommended* you use this command very often. By copying from one disk to another, it is possible that any bad sectors on the target disk (those normally bypassed by formatting) will be overwritten during DISKCOPY. If you execute DISKCOPY, you should also execute DISKCOMP to verify the disks are identical. Refer to the DOS Manual for more information.

FIND Command

Format: **[d:]FIND "text" [d:][filename[.ext]]**

The **FIND command** searches files for a given string of characters. It displays on the monitor all lines from the specified file(s) that contain the specified text. The text entered must be enclosed in a set of double quote marks. Global characters are not allowed in this command, but you may enter as many files as you wish to, separating each with a delimiter (a space).

This command has some options, such as counting the number of lines containing the text or displaying the relative line number of each matching line. For more information about these options and the FIND command itself, consult the DOS Manual.

Examples of usage:

> A> **FIND "Harvard" a:coll.doc b:filea.txt** (displays all lines in the files specified that contain the word Harvard, but *not* HARVARD or harvard)

A> **FIND** "*.*" **B:DOC** (displays all lines in B:DOS.DOC that contain the string of three characters "*.*")

FORMAT Command

Format: **[d:]FORMAT** **[d:] [/S] [/V]**

The **FORMAT command** prepares a disk in the designated drive to record data acceptable to DOS. It also examines the disk for defective sectors, making a permanent note in the File Allocation Table of the sectors that are not acceptable for recording data. If you wish to make the designated disk a "bootable" disk, use the /S option. It formats the disk and copies three system files, IBMBIO.COM, IBMDOS.COM, and COMMAND.COM, from the PC-DOS disk. In MS-DOS, the three system files are named IO.SYS, MSDOS.SYS, and COMMAND.COM.

To uniquely identify each disk, use the /V option. This option gives the formatted disk an internal volume label, consisting of from 1 to 11 characters. You can later change a volume label with the LABEL command.

All disks must be formatted before they can be used by DOS. Whenever you format a disk, all previously recorded data is destroyed. FORMAT produces a status report, indicating the following statistics for the disk just formatted: total disk space, space marked as defective, space allocated to the system files (when /S is used), and the amount of space left for your files.

Examples of usage:

A> **FORMAT b:/s** (format the disk in Drive B so that it contains the system files, making it bootable)
A> **format /s/v** (format the disk in the default drive to include the system files and a volume label)
B> **a:Format** (format the disk in Drive B)

LABEL (Volume Label) Command

Format: **[d:]LABEL** **[d:] [volume label]**

The **LABEL command** allows you to create, change, or delete a volume label on a disk. It is a good idea to internally label your disks so you can identify them using the VOL command without having to physically remove the disk from a drive. Volume labels may be up to 11 characters long. If you do not specify a label, the system will display the current label, if any. It then prompts you to enter a label, or press the Enter key to delete an existing label.

Examples of usage:

    A> **Label   b: Fred** (creates a volume label of "Fred" on Drive B)
    A> **LABEL** (displays the current volume label on the default Drive and prompts you to modify it)

RECOVER Command

Format: **[d:]RECOVER [d:]filename[.ext]** or **[d:]RECOVER d:**

The **RECOVER command** lets you reconstruct files from a disk that has a defective sector or sectors. You can recover a file containing a bad sector, minus the data in the bad sector, by using the first format of RECOVER. In addition, you can recover all files on a disk if the directory has been damaged, by using the second format of RECOVER. The second format of RECOVER *should only be used* if the directory of the disk has become unusable. Recovered files may need editing to return them to their original, corrected state.

Use of the RECOVER command with no parameters causes DOS to read the disk and recreate the FAT and the directory. It generates unique filenames in the form of FILEn.REC, where "n" is a consecutive number beginning with one. It is up to you to figure out the original filenames, however. You might try comparing file sizes from previous directory listings and using the TYPE command to display the content of listable files.

Examples of usage:

    A> **RECOVER   b:pgm.bas** (recovers a file called pgm.bas on Drive B)
    A> **recover   b:** (recovers directory for disk on Drive B)

SYS (System) Command

Format: [d:]SYS   [d:]

The **SYS command** transfers the system files (i.e., IBMBIO.COM and IBMDOS.COM in PC-DOS) from the first drive designated to the second drive designated. If you do not specify the first drive, the default drive is assumed by DOS. It will not transfer the COMMAND.COM file, however. If required, you must transfer COMMAND.COM onto the disk with the COPY command.

Typically, the SYS command is used to transfer a copy of your operating system files to a distribution program disk designed to use DOS, but sold without it. In this case, space at the beginning of the disk would have already been allocated by the manufacturer via formatting with the /B option. The SYS command transfers your hidden system files to the allocated space, thereby making it "bootable."

With SYS, you do not have to reformat your fixed disk when you upgrade from one version of DOS to a higher one. Just boot the new version from floppy disk, and then use SYS to transfer the new version's hidden files to the fixed disk. Then, copy the COMMAND.COM file and the rest of the new version commands to the fixed disk. You should make sure that no older versions of the COMMAND.COM file remain on your fixed disk, or you might get a DOS error message relating to an "Incorrect Version."

Examples of usage:

A> **SYS b:** (transfers your system files to the disk in Drive B)
A> **sys** (transfers your system files to the disk in Drive A)

Review Questions for Chapter 4:

1. What distinguishes external commands from internal commands?
2. What command is used to set a file to "read-only" status?
3. How can you view the "read-only" status of files on a disk?
4. What are the typical hidden files on a system disk?
5. How can you determine the amount of file fragmentation on a disk?
6. What command can be used to fix a corrupted FAT?
7. What command can be used to list just the filenames on a disk?

8. Why would it be beneficial for the COMP command to prompt you for filenames?
9. What command is used to see if two disks are identical?
10. What is the primary differences between using the COPY command verses using the DISKCOPY command?
11. What command is used to display the lines of a file called "B:WORK.TXT" containing the string of characters "Rbt. Smith"?
12. How do you make a disk bootable?
13. What is the purpose of a status report when formatting a disk?
14. Why would you want to use an internal volume label?
15. How can the internal volume label be changed?
16. When you reconstruct files from a disk with defective sectors, what must you typically do before you attempt to use them?
17. What happens when you use the RECOVER command without any parameters?
18. What files are transferred to an existing disk with the SYS command?
19. Why would you likely use the SYS command?
20. What would be contained in a file called FILE0001.CHK?

DOS Lab Exercise #3

1. Boot DOS (Drive A) and insert your data disk into Drive B. Enter **DIR B:** to verify the contents of Drive B. To set a file to a "read-only" status, enter **ATTRIB +R B:TEST.3** To verify that it was changed correctly, enter **ATTRIB B:TEST.*** If done correctly, TEST.1 and TEST.4 will not indicate a "read-only" status and TEST.3 will show as a "read-only" file. An "R" is displayed to the left of "read-only" filenames. Figure 4-1 shows you what the screen should look like at this point in the exercise.

72 EXTERNAL FLOPPY DISK COMMANDS

```
A>dir b:

Volume in drive B is DATA DISK
Directory of  B:\

COMMAND  COM    23210   3-07-85   1:43p
TEST     1      23210   3-07-85   1:43p
READ     ME       236   9-25-87   2:38p
TEST     3      23210   3-07-85   1:43p
TEST     4        473  10-03-87   2:18p
         5 File(s)    250880 bytes free

A>attrib +r b:test.3

A>attrib b:test.*
         B:\TEST.1
    R    B:\TEST.3
         B:\TEST.4

A>
```

Figure 4-1 Screen Display

2. To see if two files you previously created in exercise #2 are equal, enter: **COMP B:TEST.1 B:TEST.3**   If they indicate not being equal, you may have made a keying error. If you were comparing COM, EXE, or SYS files, you would get the following error message: "EOF mark not found."
3. To give a disk on Drive B a volume label, enter **LABEL B:** and follow the system prompts to enter a label of up to 11 characters (i.e., DATADISK). Enter **VOL B:** to verify the new volume label. Does your DOS disk have a volume label? Use the VOL command to check, but don't try to write one if the DOS disk you are using is not your own, or is write-protected.
4. To display all of the lines in a file that contains a given string of characters (i.e., "delimiter"), use the FIND command.   Enter **FIND "delimiter" B:READ.ME**   If you correctly entered the text in exercise #1, only one line of text should be displayed containing the string of characters "delimiter." Figure 4-2 shows you the results of executing FIND.

```
A>find "delimeter" b:read.me
---------- b:read.me
A>
```

Figure 4-2 Screen Display

5. Enter **CHKDSK** to get a status report of the default drive (A:). Then, enter **CHKDSK B:*.*** to get a status report of your data disk, directing the system to check for any fragmented files. Figure 4-3 shows you the display screen after running CHKDSK. Your display screen should look similiar to this one.

```
A>chkdsk b:*.*
Volume DATADISK    created Jan 4, 1980 12:05a

   362496 bytes total disk space
    38912 bytes in 3 hidden files
    72704 bytes in 5 user files
   250880 bytes available on disk

   655360 bytes total memory
   609232 bytes free

B:\TEST.1
   Contains 2 non-contiguous blocks.

A>
```

Figure 4-3 Screen Display

6. Change the current DOS prompt to display an added message and the system date: enter **PROMPT It is dg What is your command?** Execute a

few commands (such as DIR, VOL, and VER) to see the effect of the new system prompt. Then, return the system prompt back to normal by entering **PROMPT ng** Figure 4-4 shows you the effect of experimenting with the PROMPT command.

```
A>PROMPT It is $d$g  What is your command?

It is Thu 10-01-1987>  What is your command?dir b:

 Volume in drive B is DATADISK
 Directory of B:\

COMMAND  COM     23210   3-07-85   1:43p
TEST     1       23210   3-07-85   1:43p
READ     ME        236   9-25-87   2:38p
TEST     3       23210   3-07-85   1:43p
TEST     4         473  10-03-87   2:18p
     5 File(s)     250880 bytes free

It is Thu 10-01-1987>  What is your command?vol B:

 Volume in drive B is DATADISK

It is Thu 10-01-1987>  What is your command?ver

IBM Personal Computer DOS Version 3.10

It is Thu 10-01-1987>  What is your command?prompt $n$g
A>
```

Figure 4-4 Screen Display

7. Use **CHKDSK with the /V option** to get a listing of all the files on your DOS disk. Then use the same command to view the files on your data disk.

This concludes lab exercise #3. If time permits, experiment further with the external commands in Chapter 4. When you are finished, remove the disks and turn off the computer.

Chapter 5

FIVE IMPORTANT CONCEPTS

BATCH FILES
REDIRECTION
PIPING
EDLIN
DOS EDITING KEYS

5
Chapter

FIVE IMPORTANT CONCEPTS

This chapter introduces you to five different DOS concepts that can be very helpful to you. The first concept is the use of batch files, which allow you to automatically execute one or more DOS commands sequentially. Redirection, another important concept covered in this chapter, is the technique used for changing the standard input or output device of a DOS command, adding more flexibility to your commands. Closely related to redirection is piping, a method of transferring the output of one command to the input of another, giving you a way to combine DOS commands. Yet another item of importance to DOS users is the EDLIN line editor, which you can use to create and maintain batch files.

This chapter also covers the use of the DOS editing keys, which let you quickly make changes to the last command entered or to an EDLIN line of text, without having to re-enter keystrokes.

BATCH FILES

Batch files are one of the most useful and powerful features of DOS. If you want the computer to perform a repeated, standard task or a set of DOS commands, you do not have to enter the commands every time you want to perform that task. With batch files, you don't have to duplicate your effort. When you create a batch file consisting of DOS commands, those commands can be sequentially executed by simply typing the batch file name. This concept works the same way as an external command. Whenever you enter the name of an external command, such as FORMAT or CHKDSK, DOS goes looking for it on the appropriate disk.

To give you a good idea of how batch file processing works, let's suppose you were tired of having to enter CHKDSK every time you wanted DOS to display a status report. You could create a simple batch file called C.BAT that would enable you to execute the CHKDSK command by entering C, your batch file name. You could use the COPY command to create the batch file as follows, remembering to press the Enter key after each line of instruction keyed:

COPY CON C.BAT
CHKDSK
<F6>

Now, whenever you wanted to execute the CHKDSK command (for the default drive), you only need to enter **C** to execute the batch file. This may not seem like a big deal, yet it reduces the number of keystrokes for the CHKDSK command considerably.

But what if you wanted to get a CHKDSK status report for Drive B? Since many DOS commands must work with variable parameters, a batch file feature lets you substitute variable data into batch files. Batch files utilize a special symbol, "%n", that allows variable data to be substituted in its place. You may often need more than one variable parameter in batch files, so a number (ranging from 1 to 9) is used after the percent sign (%) to indicate which parameter is used.

The batch file above (C.BAT) could have been just as easily created with a **replaceable parameter** (%1) that would allow you to designate a particular disk drive when you executed the batch file. You would need to change the command CHKDSK (in the batch file) to **CHKDSK %1**. Then, whenever the batch file is executed, the disk drive would be included as a parameter to be substituted for the %1 entry in the batch file. For example, you could enter **C B:** to display a CHKDSK status report for Drive B. The variable "B:" would be *substituted* for "%1" in the batch file during executing of the CHKDSK command. Likewise, **C A:** would cause the batch file to execute the CHKDSK command for Drive A.

The following batch file (called COPYTXT.BAT) would allow you to make a backup copy of any .TXT file you chose and obtain a directory listing to visually verify that the copy was completed:

COPY   %2%1.TXT   %3%1.BAK
DIR   %3 /P

This batch file looks a lot more complicated than the previous example because it contains 3 replaceable parameters:

%1 represents the filename to be copied.
%2 represents the disk drive of the *original* file.
%3 represents the disk drive of the *new* file.

If you wanted to make a backup copy of BUDGET.TXT on Drive A by copying it to Drive B with a new extension of .BAK, you could enter:

COPYTXT   BUDGET   A: B:

The three parameters supplied with the batch file name during execution of the batch file ("BUDGET", "A:", and "B:") would be substituted for the replaceable parameters (%1, %2, and %3) in the batch file. In effect, the batch file commands would become:

COPY   A:BUDGET.TXT   B:BUDGET.BAK
DIR   B: /P

Immediately after DOS is booted, a ROM chip searches for an AUTOEXEC.BAT file on the system disk. If found, it will execute the predefined DOS commands contained in that file. Additionally, it will bypass the automatic prompting for DATE and TIME. You can add these commands to your AUTOEXEC.BAT file, or you can set the correct date and time from a battery-powered clock, assuming one is installed on your system.

Suppose you were setting up an office accounting system that required a specific set of tasks to be done whenever the system was booted. You could create an AUTOEXEC.BAT file, appropriately named for the term AUTOmatic EXECution, containing the specific DOS commands you require. The computer would then execute these commands each time the system was turned on. This approach would greatly simplify and standardize the startup procedures for your accounting system. Chapter 7 examines other uses of the AUTOEXEC.BAT file.

Besides the normal DOS commands available for use in batch files, several unique commands improve the power and usefulness of batch file processing. This text will not cover all of these specific commands. However, it will introduce you to three very useful batch file commands: REM, PAUSE, and ECHO.

The **REM (or remark) command** allows you to document your batch files, making them more readable. It also allows you to put messages into your batch files for other users. As you will see later, these remarks can be displayed on the screen during execution, or shown only when the batch file is displayed with the TYPE command. If you wanted to direct an inexperienced operator to insert a specific disk during the processing of a batch file, you could include the following command in the batch file:

REM INSERT THE DATA DISK INTO DRIVE B AND PRESS ENTER

However, the operator would not have time to read the message, much less take the appropriate action, before the next batch file command was executed. Fortunately, DOS provides a method for pausing execution long enough to allow you to do something before continuing. The command used is logically named **PAUSE**. Whenever the **PAUSE command** executes, it halts execution until you signal it to continue. It will automatically display the message: "**Strike a key when ready...**" on the screen.

Another batch file command used to improve communication during execution is the **ECHO command**. It has several variations. If you put the command ECHO OFF in your batch file, DOS will not display (or echo) any of the batch file commands that follow it during execution. This situation can be reversed at any time. If you put ECHO ON in your batch file, all subsequent commands (including REMs) will be displayed on the screen during execution.

If you use the ECHO command with a message after it, that message will be displayed, even if you had previously indicated ECHO OFF. An example of a batch file that uses several of these commands is provided in Figure 5-1.

```
ECHO OFF
REM  BATCH FILE NAMED L.BAT
ECHO PROCEDURE TO EXECUTE LOTUS 1-2-3
ECHO PLACE THE LOTUS DATA DISK IN DRIVE B
PAUSE
LOTUS
```

Figure 5-1 Sample Batch File (L.BAT)

To execute the sample batch file in Figure 5-1, you would enter the batch file name (L) without the extension. When DOS executes the first command in the batch file, it sets the echo mode off, such that the following REM command would not be displayed. The REM is included in the batch file for documentation purposes only. It could be displayed whenever the TYPE command is used to view the batch file contents. In that case, two ECHO messages would be displayed. Then, the system would pause, waiting for any key to be pressed before continuing to the final batch file command, the one that executes LOTUS 1-2-3. Figure 5-2 shows you what the screen displays would look like after executing the batch file.

```
A>L

A>ECHO OFF
PROCEDURE TO EXECUTE LOTUS 1-2-3
PLACE THE LOTUS DISK IN DRIVE B
Strike a key when ready . .
```

Figure 5-2 Screen Messages from the Batch File

Several fine points relating to batch files are worth mentioning:

1) If you begin a batch file statement with a *colon* (:), it will act as a remark that *only* prints when the file is displayed (i.e., using TYPE or EDLIN).

2) To issue a "beep" in a batch file (i.e., for alerting the operator of some action or problem), **ECHO <Ctrl-G>**.

3) If you enter **ECHO OFF** at the system prompt (i.e., A>) the system prompt will disappear until you enter **ECHO ON** again, or reboot the system.

4) If you press **Ctrl-C** (Ctrl-Break) when a batch file is executing, you will be prompted with a message that asks you if you wish to terminate the batch job.

5) Other batch files can be executed from within a batch file. The last command of a batch file can even be another batch file.

6) Although the COPY command (with CON) can be used to create relatively simple batch files, it cannot be used for modifying existing batch files. For this, you need some kind of text editor, like EDLIN, or a word processor.

For a more detailed explanation of batch files and additional batch file commands, refer to the DOS Manual.

REDIRECTION

Redirection is a concept of reorienting the standard input or output device used by a command to another input or output device. The standard input device is the console (or keyboard), while the standard output device is the display screen (or monitor). The "less than" sign (<) establishes a new source of input and the "greater than" sign (>) establishes a new target of output. Note: In the examples that follow, the first > is part of the system prompt.

Examples of usage:

> A> **DIR >B:DIR.LST** (redirects the output display of the DIR command away from the screen and to a file on Drive B named DIR.LST)
>
> A> **dir >prn** (directs the DIR display to go to the printer)
>
> A> **Sort <B:filea.txt > B:fileb.txt** (uses filea.txt as the input for a SORT command that outputs the sorted results to fileb.txt)

PIPING

Piping is a way of telling DOS to transfer the output from one command to be input for another command. It accomplishes this transferral by creating a temporary file on the default disk for each "piped" set of data. The first command outputs to a temporary file that is read by the second command. If the piping operation is lengthy, multiple "pipes" could be created. When the operation is completed, DOS deletes the temporary file(s). You can think of piping as a form of redirection. The major difference is that with piping, the temporary file is created by DOS and not the user.

Piping usually involves the use of special commands, termed **filters,** that accept data, do something with it, and then pass it to the next step. There are three standard filters used by DOS in piping:

FIND (used to search a file for a specified string of text)
MORE (used to display only one screen of output at a time, waiting for the user to press any key to continue)
SORT (used to sort disk filenames into a desired sequence)

The symbol used by DOS to indicate a piping operation is the vertical bar (|). The standard output device for both the DIR and SORT command is the monitor. If you "pipe" the output from a DIR command into the SORT command, then the output displayed on the monitor will be the sorted listing of the directory. For example:

DIR | SORT

The above example is equivalent to the following set of commands:

DIR> A:TEMPFILE.$$$
A:TEMPFILE.$$$< SORT
DEL A:TEMPFILE.$$$

If you find that the sorted directory is too large to fit on a single screen, you can "pipe" to an additional command as follows:

DIR | SORT | MORE

Figure 5-3 shows you what the first page might look like when the above command is executed. The two strangely named files at the beginning of the directory are temporary files used by the piping process. DOS will automatically delete them at the end of the piping process. Obviously, the default drive disk must not be write-protected and there must be room for these temporary files to be written.

```
        40 File(s)     41984 bytes free
  Directory of    A:\
  Volume in drive A is DOS DISK
  0C2E331E              0    10-04-87   12:46p
  0C2E3454              0    10-04-87   12:46p
  ANSI      SYS      1651     3-07-85    1:43p
  ASSIGN    COM      1509     3-07-85    1:43p
  ATTRIB    EXE     15091     3-07-85    1:43p
  BACKUP    COM      5377     3-07-85    1:43p
  BASIC     COM     17792     3-07-85    1:43p
  BASICA    COM     27520     3-07-85    1:43p
  CHKDSK    COM      9435     3-07-85    1:43p
  COMMAND   COM     23210     3-07-85    1:43p
  COMP      COM      3664     3-07-85    1:43p
  CONFIG    SYS        40     9-17-87    6:10p
  DEBUG     COM     15552     3-07-85    1:43p
  DISKCOMP  COM      4073     3-07-85    1:43p
  DISKCOPY  COM      4329     3-07-85    1:43p
  EDLIN     COM      7261     3-07-85    1:43p
  FDISK     COM      8173     3-07-85    1:43p
  FIND      EXE      6403     3-07-85    1:43p
  FORMAT    COM      9398     3-07-85    1:43p
  -- More --
```

Figure 5-3 Screen Display

If you want to display a directory of files that were created on a given date, you can use the piping concept as follows:

DIR | FIND "11-16-86"

Likewise, if you wanted a directory of files with an extension of .DOC, you could enter:

DIR | FIND "DOC"

In this example, FIND would not be able to locate any files on the directory listing with ".DOC", because directory listings do not contain the period before the extension. In addition, it would not find any extensions of "doc", because directory listings only contain upper-case filenames.

Piping and redirection can be combined in a single operation. If you wanted a sorted directory listing to be saved on a file called B:SORTED.DIR, you could enter the following:

DIR | SORT >B:SORTED.DIR

Sometimes it is useful to display data from a listable file on the screen, but only one screenful at a time. If you wanted to display a large file, i.e., B:ACCOUNT.TXT, on the screen, you could enter:

MORE <B:ACCOUNT.TXT

This command would direct MORE to get its input from B:ACCOUNT.TXT. Unless otherwise directed, MORE sends its output to the monitor one screenful at a time.

The use of redirection and piping, including filters, can be quite useful once you understand how to use them.

EDLIN

EDLIN is a limited DOS line editor that should greatly facilitate the creation and modification of batch files. EDLIN contains its own set of one-letter commands, which enable you to create and save files such as batch files; update and edit existing files; and search, delete, or replace multiple lines or characters of text. You can use EDLIN as a rudimentary word processor. However, since EDLIN is line-oriented, it is not applicable for the typical memo or document. Line numbers are included for reference only, and are only displayed by EDLIN. Line numbers are never saved with the file. When you add or delete lines of text, the line numbers are *automatically updated* by EDLIN. If you refer to a line number greater than the highest line number in the text, EDLIN will substitute the highest number for the one referenced.

When you see an asterisk displayed, it denotes the **current line** which helps you keep track of where you are in an EDLIN file. With EDLIN, you can refer to line numbers relative to the current line number, the one indicated with the asterisk. Use the + or - with a number to indicate a relative line number either before (-) or ahead (+) of the current line number. For example, if the current line number is 17 and you want to reference line number 22, use +5. You could reference line number 7 by using -10.

The format of the DOS command to execute EDLIN is as follows:

[d:]EDLIN [d:]filename[.ext]

If the file specified does not exist, EDLIN assumes you want to create a new file and displays "New file". At this point, you can enter **I** and begin entering text, line at a time. If the file specified is found, EDLIN will display "End of input file" and awaits your first command.

Although there are several other EDLIN commands, Figure 5-4 contains a summary of some of the most often used EDLIN commands, with an accompanying explanation of each. These commands are entered at the EDLIN prompt (*). The general form of an EDLIN command is a line number (or range of numbers), followed immediately by an EDLIN command. In some cases, these single letter commands include optional parameters, that must be separated with either a period or a comma. Commands may be entered using both upper and lower case characters.

> **C (Copy lines)** - copies a range of lines to a specified line number, where the copied lines are placed just prior to the specified line. For example, to copy lines 2 through 7 and place them before the current line 17, enter **2,7,17C**.
>
> **D (Delete lines)** - deletes a specified range of lines. For example, to delete lines 4 through 16, enter **4,16D**. To delete line 4 only, enter **4D**. Enter **D** to delete just the current line (the one denoted with the asterisk).
>
> **E (End edit)** - ends an edit session and saves the edited file. When you exit EDLIN, the original file (if any) is saved with a .BAK extension. The new modified file is saved with the name of the original file.
>
> **I (Insert lines)** - inserts lines of text immediately before the specified line. When you create a new file, you must enter **I** before you begin entering text. To exit from the insert mode, enter **<F6>** or **Ctrl-Break**. For example, to begin inserting lines of text before the current line 15, enter **15I**.

L (List lines) - displays lines of text from the file based on a specified range of lines. For example, to display lines 16-19, enter **16,19L**. To display the 23 lines that surround the current line, enter **L**. To display a total of 23 lines starting with line 34, enter **34L**.

M (Move lines) - moves a specified range of lines immediately before a specified line. For example, to move lines 14-27 immediately before the current line 4, enter **14,27,4M**.

P (Page) - display 23 lines at a time from the current line, making the last line listed the new current line.

Q (Quit edit) - quits the editing session *without* saving any changes.

R (Replace text) - replaces all occurences of a text string with another text string. For example, to change each occurence of the word "MS-DOS" to "PC-DOS" in the first 25 lines of text, enter **1,25RMS-DOS<F6>PC-DOS**, where <F6> is the F6 function key, that must be entered between the two strings of text.

S (Search text) - searches the file beginning with a specified line, to locate a specified text string. For example, to search the entire file for all occurrences of "PC-DOS", enter **1SPC-DOS**. The search command allows you to continue locating all occurrences of the specified string until the "Not found" message is displayed.

Figure 5-4 Summary of EDLIN Commands (Part 2)

A line number by itself can also be entered as a command. The line number directs EDLIN to display the contents of that line and allow you to change it on the line below where it is displayed. In addition, that line now becomes the current line number. If you enter a new line of text, it will replace the old text as soon as you press the Enter key. You may also use the DOS editing keys (see below) to quickly make changes within the existing line of text. Characters to the right of the cursor when the Enter key is pressed are erased. Prior to pressing the Enter key, however, you can press either **Esc** (Escape) or **Ctrl-Break** to cancel any changes to that line.

In the event that not enough primary memory is available to load the entire file being edited (leaving 25% of the loaded file size for modifications) you will not get any message displayed. If this situation occurs, you will need to refer to the DOS Manual for a description of the two applicable commands, Append Lines and Write Lines.

DOS EDITING KEYS

Frequently, you will need to make minor modifications to either a line of text (for instance, in EDLIN) or a command line in a batch file. Rather than having to rekey the entire line you just entered incorrectly, the **DOS editing keys** allow you to change only the characters that require modification.

Whenever you enter a line, DOS puts a copy of the line in a temporary storage location, called an **input buffer,** so you can recall it and make modifications without duplicating keystrokes. The DOS editing keys are used to display the line currently stored in the input buffer (i.e., the *last* line entered) and to edit that line.

You can also use DOS editing keys to modify the last command entered from the keyboard. The process of modifying involves inserting or deleting one or more characters in the line. You cannot just type over existing characters using the DOS editing keys. Figure 5-5 is a summary of the DOS editing keys that you should find most helpful to you.

- **F1 -** Display one character at a time from the buffer. (You can use the right-arrow key to do the same thing).
- **F2 x -** Display all characters in the buffer up to the given character (x).
- **F3 -** Display all characters in the buffer.
- **F4 x -** Delete all characters in the buffer up to the given character (x).
- **F5 -** Update the buffer with the changes as displayed.
- **INS -** Insert one or more characters in the buffer at the cursor location.
- **DEL -** Delete a character at a time from the buffer.
- **Esc -** Escape (cancel) the operation, leaving the input buffer unchanged.

Figure 5-5 Summary of DOS Editing Keys

Perhaps the best way to understand how to use the DOS editing keys is by example. The situations that follow demonstrate what you can do using the DOS editing keys; practice these examples to reinforce what you've learned thus far.

I. Suppose you entered **COPY A:TEST1.XT B:TEST1.BAK** and got an error message because TEST1.XT was not found on Drive A (i.e., it was misspelled in the command). To correct:
   1) Press **F2 X** to move the cursor to the period just before the "X", displaying COPY A:TEST1.
   2) Press **INS** and the letter "T".
   3) Press **F3** to display the rest of the buffer. Now it shows as **COPY   A:TEST1.TXT   B:TEST1.BAK**
   4) Press **ENTER** to execute the command and get back to the system prompt.

II. Suppose you entered **COPY A:TEST3.DOC   B:TEST.BAK** and wanted to redo it because you intended to enter B:TEST3.BAK. To correct:
   1) Press **F3** to display all of the input buffer.
   2) Use the **Backarrow key** to delete the last four characters (i.e., .BAK).
   3) Re-enter **3.BAK** and press the **Enter key**.

III. Suppose you entered **TYPE B:TEST3.DOC** and got what you wanted, but now you also want to display **B:TEST2.DOC**.
   1) Press **F1** until the "3" in the filename is displayed.
   2) Press **DEL** to delete the "3".
   3) Press **INS** and a "**2**" to replace the "3" that was deleted.
   4) Press **F3** to finish displaying the buffer and **Enter**.

Review Questions for Chapter 5

1. What is the purpose of batch files?
2. How are batch files identified by DOS?
3. What are two typical methods for creating batch files?
4. How is variable data (parameters) included in batch files?
5. When is an AUTOEXEC.BAT file executed?
6. Why are REM statements used in batch files?
7. When are REM statements in batch files displayed?
8. What is the function of a PAUSE statement in a batch file?
9. What happens when you enter **ECHO OFF** at the system prompt?
10. What is the standard input device in DOS?
11. What is the standard output device in DOS?

12. How would you use redirection to print a directory listing?
13. What kind of file is created with "piping"?
14. What is the purpose of the MORE filter?
15. Why would the command **DIR | FIND ".COM"** *not* yield any output?
16. What is the dual purpose of the asterisk (*) in EDLIN?
17. What does the EDLIN command **6,12D** accomplish?
18. What happens when you exit EDLIN with the command "E"?
19. When can DOS editing keys be used?
20. What DOS editing key displays all the characters in the buffer?

DOS Lab Exercise #4

1. For this exercise, you will be creating some temporary files on the DOS disk, so you should remove any write protect tab that is on the disk first. Boot DOS (Drive A) and insert your data disk in Drive B. Then, enter **DIR B:** To experiment with redirection and piping, enter the following:

   DIR >B:TEST1.DIR (to redirect directory from the monitor to a file named TEST1.DIR)
   SORT <B:TEST1.DIR >B:TEST2.DIR (to sort the previously created file and redirect it to another filename)
   DIR | SORT (to list the sorted directory of default disk)
   DIR B: | SORT (to list a sorted directory of Drive B -- the screen should look like Figure 5-6)

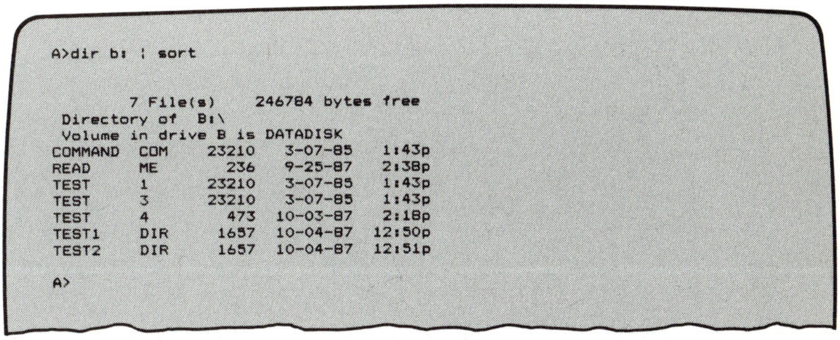

```
A>dir b: | sort


        7 File(s)     246784 bytes free
 Directory of  B:\
 Volume in drive B is DATADISK
COMMAND   COM     23210   3-07-85   1:43p
READ      ME        236   9-25-87   2:38p
TEST      1       23210   3-07-85   1:43p
TEST      3       23210   3-07-85   1:43p
TEST      4         473  10-03-87   2:18p
TEST1     DIR      1657  10-04-87  12:50p
TEST2     DIR      1657  10-04-87  12:51p

A>
```

Figure 5-6 Screen Display

        DIR | SORT > B:TEST3.DIR (output sorted directory to a file)
        TYPE   B:TEST3.DIR | MORE (display a file, screen at a time)

Figure 5-7 shows you what the screen might look like after executing the last TYPE command and displaying the last screen.

92   FIVE IMPORTANT CONCEPTS

```
     40 File(s)      41984 bytes free
  Directory of  A:\
  Volume in drive A is DOS DISK
 0C361A4A              0   10-04-87   12:54p
 0C361C17              0   10-04-87   12:54p
 ANSI     SYS       1651    3-07-85    1:43p
 ASSIGN   COM       1509    3-07-85    1:43p
 ATTRIB   EXE      15091    3-07-85    1:43p
 BACKUP   COM       5577    3-07-85    1:43p
 BASIC    COM      17792    3-07-85    1:43p
 BASICA   COM      27520    3-07-85    1:43p
 CHKDSK   COM       9435    3-07-85    1:43p
 COMMAND  COM      23210    3-07-85    1:43p
 COMP     COM       3664    3-07-85    1:43p
 CONFIG   SYS         40    9-17-87    6:10p
 DEBUG    COM      15552    3-07-85    1:43p
 DISKCOMP COM       4073    3-07-85    1:43p
 DISKCOPY COM       4329    3-07-85    1:43p
 EDLIN    COM       7261    3-07-85    1:43p
 FDISK    COM       8173    3-07-85    1:43p
 FIND     EXE       6403    3-07-85    1:43p
 FORMAT   COM       9398    3-07-85    1:43p
 -- More --
```

Figure 5-7 Screen Display

2. If you are currently connected to a printer, you can complete this portion of the lab exercise. Otherwise, just read through it and use your imagination. To print a sorted directory listing on the printer, rather than on the monitor, enter:

   DIR | SORT > PRN

   To print a sorted directory of just those filenames on Drive B with a filename containing "test" on the printer, enter:

   DIR B: | FIND "TEST" | SORT > PRN

3. Create a single command batch file that will automatically sort the directory of files on the default drive into alphabetical sequence, before displaying it one screen at a time:

**COPY CON ASORT.BAT
DIR | SORT | MORE
\<F6\>**

Enter the batch file name of **ASORT** to get a sorted directory of the default drive, one screen at a time. The output should look like what you displayed from the last command in Part 1 (Figure 5-7), except that this directory includes ASORT.BAT.

Before you continue to the next exercise, please remember to delete ASORT.BAT from the default drive (i.e., **DEL ASORT.BAT**).

4. Set up a batch file to prevent anyone from formatting a disk on Drive A by mistake. This batch file will only permit FORMAT to format a disk on Drive B. Enter:

**RENAME FORMAT.COM FORMATB.COM
COPY CON FORMAT.BAT
FORMATB B:
\<F6\>**

Notice that the original FORMAT command had to be renamed so you could use FORMAT as the new batch file name. Then, the batch file was used to execute the renamed format command with the desired option, the formatting of Drive B only.

Remove the disk in Drive B and enter **FORMAT** to execute the batch file just created. When you get the message to insert a blank disk in Drive B, you can press Ctrl-Break to escape from completing the execution of this command. Figure 5-8 shows you what the screen should look like after terminating the batch file named FORMAT.BAT.

94 FIVE IMPORTANT CONCEPTS

```
A>del asort.bat

A>rename format.com formatb.com

A>copy con format.bat
formatb b:
^Z
        1 File(s) copied

A>format

A>formatb b:
Insert new diskette for drive B:
and strike ENTER when ready^C

Terminate batch job (Y/N)? y
A>
```

Figure 5-8 Screen Display

Before you continue to the next step, don't forget to delete FORMAT.BAT and then rename FORMATB.COM to FORMAT.COM. Can you think of any other useful commands you would like to create?

5. Use **COPY CON AUTOEXEC.BAT** to create a batch file on your DOS disk containing the following commands:

```
REM SAMPLE INITIALIZATION PROCEDURE
ECHO OFF
DATE
TIME
ECHO ON
PAUSE  PLACE DATA DISK IN DRIVE B
DIR A: >B:DISKA.DIR
DIR B:
REM  END OF INITIALIZATION
ECHO OFF
```

ECHO HAVE A NICE DAY
PROMPT DATE IS $D TIME IS $T $_WHAT NEXT?

Don't forget to press F6 and Enter key to cause these commands to be written to the AUTOEXEC.BAT file. If you make an error after you pressed the Enter key on any line, you will have to cancel the process with Ctrl-Break, and re-do the COPY from the beginning. When you are done, do a warm boot (Ctrl-Alt-Del) to boot DOS and have this new batch file automatically executed.

Experiment entering a few commands (i.e., TIME, VER, and VOL) with the new prompt. To change back to the original prompt, enter **PROMPT**.

When you are finished, copy AUTOEXEC.BAT to Drive B and then delete it from the DOS disk. If you previously removed the write-protect tab on the DOS disk, put it back on, covering the write-protect notch. This is the end of lab exercise #4. Don't forget to remove the disks and turn off the computer when you are done.

DOS Lab Exercise #5

1. *This exercise is best accomplished if done in class as a group.*
   Experiment with "beginning" EDLIN commands, such as Insert, Delete, List, Quit, and End. For this part of the exercise, boot DOS, place your data disk in Drive B, and enter:

   EDLIN B:LINEDIT.DOC

   Now enter the following commands (comments in parenthesis):

   I (begin inserting lines of text)
   ONE (this is the first line of text)
   TWO
   THREE
   . (continue up to TEN)
   TEN
   Ctrl-Brk or <F6> (to end entering lines of text)

96 FIVE IMPORTANT CONCEPTS

       L (list the lines of text entered)
       4D (delete line four of the text)
       L (list text again to verify deletion)
       10I (insert 10 lines of text before line 10)
       ELEVEN (this is the first line of text to be added)
       TWELVE (this is the last line of text)
       Ctrl-Brk or <F6> (stop inserting text)
       L (list text as it now stands)
       4 (display line 4 and allow it to be changed)
       FOUR (change previous text in line 4 to "FOUR")
       L (verify change)
       5I (insert text before line 5)
       FIVE (text to be inserted)
       Ctrl-Brk or <F6> (stop inserting text)
       4,8L (list only lines 4 through 8)
       10,12D (delete lines 10 through 12)
       Q (instruct EDLIN to quit without saving changes)
       N (abort the quit - ie. you entered Q by mistake)
       E (instruct EDLIN to exit saving the changes)

2. Experiment with DOS editing keys by entering the following:
    a) **DIR A:** (pressing Enter to execute this command)
       DIR A: /P (using F3 to allow you to easily add the "/p")
    b) **COPY B:TEST3.DR B:TEST3.BAK** (using no editing keys)
       COPY B:TEST3.DIR B:TEST3.BAK (using the DOS editing keys to make corrections to previous entry)
    c) **EDLIN B:LINEDIT.DOC** (recall previous text file)
       6I (enter the insert mode)
       NOW IS THE TIME FOR ALL GOOD WOMEN TO LEARN COMPUTERS.
       <F6> (end inserting text)
       6 (list line 6 and allow for change)
       <F1>...<F1> (press F1 *29 times* until just before the "W" in WOMEN would have been displayed)
       <DEL> <DEL> (press DEL *twice* to delete "WO" in buffer)
       <F3> (display the remainder of the buffer)
       L (list the file to verify the change)
       Q (quit EDLIN)
       Y (respond "Y" to verify the abort)

3. Experiment with "more advanced" EDLIN Commands, such as Copy, Move, Replace, Search, and Transfer. Enter the following:
    EDLIN B:LINEDIT.DOC (to retrieve the file previously created)
    L (list the file to refresh your memory)
    1,5,10C (copy lines 1 - 5 before line 10)
    7,11,14C (copy lines 7 - 11 before line 14)
    1L (list lines of text beginning with line 1)
    1,19RTWO<F6>TO (in lines 1 - 19, replace every occurrence of "TWO" with "TO")
    1L (list lines of text to verify change)
    9,19SFIVE (in lines 9 - 19, search for and locate "FIVE")
    18TB:READ.ME (at line 18, transfer a file called READ.ME)
    1L (list text)
    15I (begin inserting before line 15)
    SIX (line of text to be inserted)
    Ctrl-Brk or <F6> (stop inserting)
    1L (list text)
    16L (list text beginning with line 16)
    18 (list line 18 and allow for changes to that line)
    <F1><F1><F1> (depress F1 three times to display the first three characters of line 18)
    TH (add two more characters to that line)
    15L (list lines of text beginning with line 15)
    E (exit EDLIN and save changes to data disk)

4. Delete the AUTOEXEC.BAT file on Drive B that you created with COPY CON in Lab Exercise #4. Use EDLIN to recreate it.

5. For additional work, build a batch file on your data disk with EDLIN to create a new command for you. This batch file, called **MOVE.BAT**, will allow you to copy a file giving it another name and then delete the original name. In other words, you will be creating a modification of the "rename" command that allows you to rename a file and have the original file copied to another disk. The new batch file should contain the following:

    COPY %1 %2
    DEL %1

This new batch file will be invoked (executed) by entering the batch file name (B:MOVE) followed by two parameters (for %1 and %2). The parameter %1 represents the original filename, and %2 represents the new filename. For example:

B:MOVE   B:TEST3.DIR   B:TEST5.DIR

Once executed, B:TEST3.DIR would be renamed B:TEST5.DIR. If you had desired, you could have specified that the new file was to be created on Drive A instead of Drive B.

This ends lab exercise #5. Remove disks and turn off the computer if you are finished.

Chapter 6

FIXED DISK CONCEPTS AND COMMANDS

DIRECTORIES AND SUBDIRECTORIES
FIXED DISK COMMANDS
    FDISK Command (external)
    CD (Change Directory) Command (internal)
    MD (Make Directory) Command (internal)
    RD (Remove Directory) Command (internal)
    PATH (Set Search Directory) Command (internal)
    TREE Command (external)
    BACKUP Command (external)
    RESTORE Command (external)

6
Chapter

FIXED DISK CONCEPTS AND COMMANDS

If you have a fixed disk installed on your computer system, you will undoubtedly notice two significant improvements over floppy disk processing. First, the speed at which data can be transferred to and from fixed disks is approximately *twenty times* that of the 5 1/4-inch floppy disks. The second improvement is the amount of data that can be stored on fixed disks. A 20MB fixed disk, for example, can typically hold the equivalent of 55 or 56 floppy disks. These advantages could significantly change the way you use your computer.

The use of fixed disks creates some considerations not necessarily relevant when using floppy disks. The first consideration is the need for a good power supply that does not permit a loss of electrical power. A temporary power loss can cause the disk's read/write heads to "crash" on the surface of the fixed disk, causing permanent damage. In order to ensure continuous power, an uninterruptable power supply (UPS) is recommended for fixed disk systems. A UPS, usually costing around $400, will protect both the data stored on the disk as well as the fixed disk itself.

Another consideration is the need for periodic backup of the data stored on your fixed disk to floppy disks. Although this consideration is equally valid for data stored on floppy disks, history shows that fixed disk users tend to overlook this process. Get into the habit of backing up your fixed disks regularly. You will be glad you did the day you turn on your computer and hear a noise like a wrench in a blender.

One other consideration is the need to move the read/write heads to an unused area of the fixed disk before you "power down" the system. When the power is turned off, the read/write heads on some fixed disk drives do not retract automatically. Instead, they settle down on the surface of the fixed disk. Over time, this process can damage data stored on the disk. If you have a fixed disk that does not automatically retract the heads, or if your computer is likely to be moved while it is turned off, you should execute a program (i.e., PARK or SHIPDISK) that moves the heads to a vacant cylinder just prior to turning off the power.

DIRECTORIES AND SUBDIRECTORIES

Because large amounts of data can be stored on a fixed disk, it is extremely helpful to subdivide the total space into uniquely named areas. These areas can be reserved to store only certain groups of files, thereby allowing you to organize and classify files by area. DOS uses a **root** or **main directory** and optional **subdirectories** (directories within a directory) to keep track of the name and location of all files on disk. You can establish subdirectories for floppy disks, but the use of subdirectories is generally more practical for fixed disks.

With the release of DOS 2.x, you can organize and control hundreds of files on fixed disk by adopting a tree-structured file directory system. The root directory branches into subdirectories. The subdirectories in turn, can branch into further subdirectories in a hierarchy much like that of a family tree or an organization chart in a company. Each subdirectory is assigned a unique name using the same rules we use with filenames. With floppy disks, files are often organized manually by recording selected groups of files on a disk and identifying each disk with a label. Subdirectories provide a big advantage in that they allow you to organize all of the files on a fixed disk "electronically." Figure 6-1 shows a graphic example of a tree-structured directory.

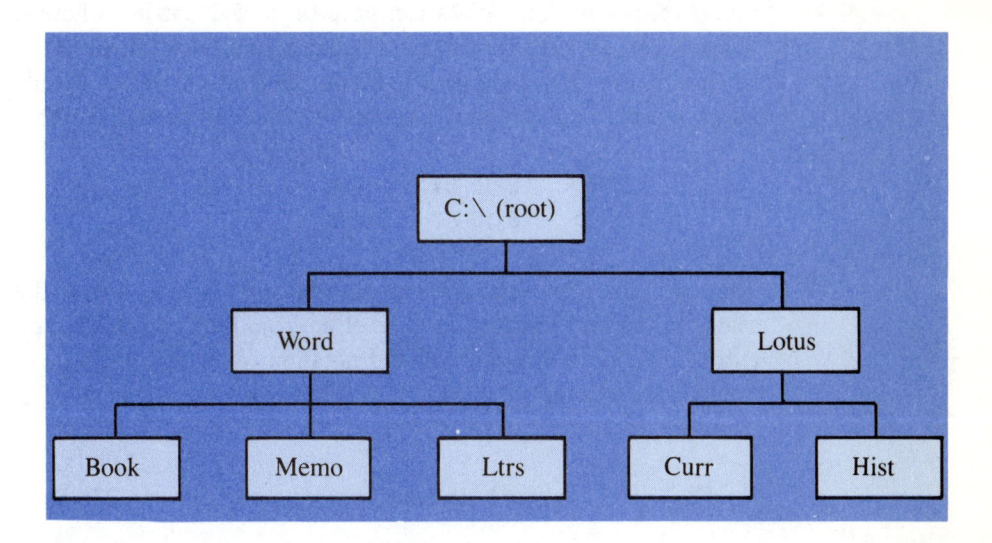

Figure 6-1 Sample Hierarchy of Subdirectories

In the sample tree structure above, the root directory is divided into two subdirectories: one for word processing and one for spreadsheets. The word processing subdirectory, WORD, is further subdivided into three subdirectories: one for a manuscript, one for memos, and one for personal letters. DOS uses the backslash (\) to identify a subdirectory name.

Thus, the filename BOSS.DOC, stored on the MEMO subdirectory, is identified with the full name C:\WORD\MEMO\BOSS.DOC. The backslash identifies a **path** of subdirectories that must be taken by DOS to find the file in the hierarchy. If the path is not included in the filename, the system will look for the file on the current directory. The backslash at the beginning of the path directs DOS to begin the path with the root directory. If it is not included, the path will begin with the current directory. If the file you need is not on the current directory, you must provide DOS the path to find it. This path must be part of the full filename, just like the disk designator is supplied when a file is not on the default drive.

DOS has a number of commands that allow you to create and use subdirectories. Any reference to the "**current directory**" refers to the subdirectory you are currently working in. You can change to another directory at any time. The root directory on fixed disks can have up to 512 entries, where entries can be filenames or subdirectory names. Subdirectories are identified on a directory listing (via the DIR command) with the symbol <DIR>. In subdirectory listings, you will see a "dot" and "double-dot" directory entries, like this:

```
.      <DIR>    8-15-87    9:45a
..     <DIR>    8-15-87    9:45a
```

The single dot represents the current directory and the double-dot entry represents the "parent" directory, one level up from the current directory. These two entries can be used as a shorthand notation when referencing a directory. For example, to change to the LOTUS\HIST directory from the LOTUS\CURR directory, enter:

CD ..\HIST (since both subdirectories are part of LOTUS)

The following helpful hints will assist you in correctly setting up the directory structure on a fixed disk:

1. Do not clutter up your root directory with lots of programs or data files. Place program files in an appropriate subdirectory. Perhaps just a few files will suffice: hidden files, COMMAND.COM, CONFIG.SYS with its required device drivers, and AUTOEXEC.BAT.
2. Do not assign extensions to your subdirectory names, as it complicates the path name unnecessarily.
3. Do not nest your subdirectories more than 2 or 3 levels below the root directory, as it makes the path name too long and cumbersome.
4. Give your subdirectories short, but meaningful names: \DOS, \UTIL, \WORD, \DB, \SS, etc. This will assist you in recall without making the path name too unwieldy.

FIXED DISK COMMANDS

Figure 6-2 lists and briefly defines eight of the commands you will be most likely to use with fixed disk systems. Each command is explained in detail in this chapter, along with examples of usage. The commands are listed and discussed in a logical sequence, rather than in alphabetical sequence, to facilitate understanding.

> **FDISK** - Fixed Disk Setup, used to divide a fixed disk into one or more separate areas (partitions).
> **CD** - Change Directory, used to change to another subdirectory or the root directory.
> **MD** - Make Directory, used to create a subdirectory.
> **RD** - Remove Directory, used to eliminate a subdirectory.
> **PATH** - Instructs DOS where to look for command files.
> **TREE** - Displays the complete directory tree structure.
> **BACKUP** - Copies fixed disk files to floppy disks.
> **RESTORE** - Restores fixed disk files from floppy disks.

Figure 6-2 Fixed Disk Command Summary

The format for all commands designated as external includes the optional parameter [d:][path] just before the command. These parameters may be used to designate the disk drive and/or the path that contains the external command.

FDISK Command (external)

Format: **FDISK (requires the DOS disk in Drive A)**

The **FDISK command** creates and manages partitions on a fixed disk. Normally, you will only have a single partition, devoted exclusively to DOS, on your fixed disk. However, the capability exists to have multiple operating systems installed on a fixed disk, in which only one can be active at any time. The FDISK command allows you to create partitions, change from one partition to another one, or delete partitions. Even if you have just one partition, you must still run FDISK to allocate all of your fixed disk to DOS.

When you first execute FDISK, chose the option that "**Creates DOS partition.**" The system will then ask you if you want to use the entire fixed disk system for DOS. If you wish to have DOS as the only operating system, respond with "Y". Otherwise, respond with "N" and consult the DOS Manual for further instructions. After the fixed disk partition is established, you must run **FORMAT** to prepare it for recording data. Run **FORMAT** with the "/S" option to place the two DOS hidden system files and COMMAND.COM on the disk.

Once these system files are transferred to the fixed disk, you can boot the system from the fixed disk. You should copy all of the DOS external commands to your fixed disk, and then put your floppy disk of DOS away for safekeeping. When you turn on the computer with a bootable fixed disk, do not have any disk in Drive A or the system will try to boot using the floppy disk.

CD (Change Directory) Command (internal) — also CHDIR

Format: **CD [d:][path]**

The **CD command** lets you change from the current subdirectory to another one. The path is used to identify the directory you want to change to. For example, if you want to change to the root directory, you enter **CD**. You can enter the CD command with no parameters to display the current directory. A leading backslash (\) in the path directs DOS to start the path at the root directory. Normally, you want to start at the root directory to make sure DOS will be able to locate the appropriate subdirectory.

Examples of usage:

> C> **CD ** (change to the root directory)
> C> **Cd** (display the current directory)
> C> **cd \word\memo** (change to the subdirectory named MEMO on the WORD subdirectory, starting from the root directory)
> C> **CD Word\MEMO** (change to the subdirectory identified as MEMO on the WORD subdirectory, starting from the current directory)
> C> **cd..** (change to the parent subdirectory)

MD (Make Directory) Command (internal) — also MKDIR

Format: **MD [d:]path**

The **MD command** creates a subdirectory in a given location. You may create as many subdirectories as you want, but keep in mind that too many could cause confusion. Each subdirectory can contain both file and subdirectory names that occur on other subdirectories, but names must be unique within a subdirectory.

Example of usage:

    C> **MD \word** (creates a subdirectory named WORD one level down from the root directory)
    C> **md \word\MEMO** (creates the subdirectory MEMO one level down from the subdirectory named WORD)
    C> **Md games** (creates a subdirectory called GAMES one level down from the current directory)

RD (Remove Directory) Command (internal) — also RMDIR

Format: **RD [d:]path**

The **RD command** removes a subdirectory from disk. However, before you can remove a subdirectory, all files within that subdirectory must be deleted and all of its subdirectories must be removed. You cannot remove the root directory or the current subdirectory.

Examples of usage:

    C> **rd \word\memo** (remove the subdirectory named MEMO from the WORD subdirectory)
    C> **RD \WORD** (remove subdirectory WORD from the root directory)

PATH (Set Search Directory) Command (internal)

Format: **PATH [d:][path][;path]**

The **PATH command** allows you to direct the system to search one or more subdirectories for commands (or batch files) not found in the current subdirectory. With a hierarchical file directory, you cannot access any command just by entering the command name. You must specify the path which DOS can locate the command if it resides on another subdirectory (other than the current directory). The PATH command instructs DOS what subdirectories to search, and in what order, to find a command that is not on the current directory. PATH only locates *command* files that can be executed. Within each directory, DOS always looks for a matching command with a .COM extension first. Then it tries the .EXE extension, and finally, the .BAT extension. (Beginning with DOS 3.2, however, the APPEND command was added to allow users to set up a search path for *data* files. Consult your DOS 3.2 manual for details.)

Typing PATH with no parameters will display the current path. Entering PATH with just a semicolon tells the system you do not want any search path. Issuing a PATH command does not change the current directory.

Examples of usage:

    C> **Path \DOS** (directs the system to look on the sub-directory named DOS, if it cannot find the desired command or batch file name on the current subdirectory)
    C> **PATH \word\ltrs** (directs the system to look on LTRS within WORD to find what it is looking for, if it is not on the current subdirectory)
    C> **path** (display the current search path setting)
    C> **Path ;** (delete any previous search path setting)
    C> **PATH \;\UTIL;\DOS** (directs DOS to search 3 directories in the order given: root, \UTIL, and \DOS)

TREE Command (external)

Format: **[d:][path]TREE [d:][/F]**

The **TREE command** displays all of the subdirectory paths on the specified drive. When the /F option is used, TREE will optionally list all the files in the root directory and each subdirectory. However, the TREE command does not yield a very readable listing with the /F option. If you don't like TREE, try using **CHKDSK /V.** It lists all files, showing the complete pathname.

Examples of usage:

    C> **TREE /f** (displays all of the subdirectories and all of the files in the root directory and each subdirectory)
    C> **tree >prn** (prints a listing of all the subdirectories)

BACKUP Command (external)

Format: **[d:][path]BACKUP   [d]:[path][filename[.ext]]   d:[/S][/M]**, where the first parameter after the command is the source drive, and the second parameter is the target.

The **BACKUP command** copies your fixed disk files to as many formatted floppy disks as are needed to hold it in a compressed form. Beginning with DOS 3.3, the disks no longer have to be previously formatted. You may include a filename with the source parameter to restrict the files you want to back up. Global characters can be used in the filename and extension. The BACKUP command provides you with many options that make it easier to control how you copy your files. You can use the /S option to copy subdirectory files, in addition to the files in specified or current directory. Use the /M option to backup only those files that have been modified since the last backup.

Whenever BACKUP fills a floppy disk, you will be prompted to insert a new diskette. Label each backup disk in consecutive order so you can restore them in the same order. **NOTE: BACKUP is not the same as COPY.** When files are recorded on disks with BACKUP, they cannot be used until they are restored to the fixed disk with the RESTORE command.

Examples of usage:

C> **BACKUP C:*.* A:/S** (backup all files on Drive C to Drive A)
C> **backup c:\word\book*.doc a:/m** (backup only files in the BOOK subdirectory within WORD that have an extension of .DOC, and have been modified since the last backup on that subdirectory)
C> **Backup C:*.txt a:/s** (backup all files on the fixed disk with an extension of .TXT)

RESTORE Command (external)

Format: **[d:][path]RESTORE   d: [d:][path]filename[.ext] [/S]**, where the first drive designator after the command is the source drive, and the second is the target drive.

The **RESTORE command** is used to restore one or more files from backup disks created with the BACKUP command. When multiple backup disks are involved, the system will prompt you to insert the next diskette. You may use the global characters for filenames and extensions with the RESTORE command.

With the /S option, this command will automatically recreate deleted subdirectories on a fixed disk if needed. Thus, RESTORE can be used, along with BACKUP, to transfer fixed disk files to another fixed disk. This feature could come in handy if you wanted to restore your backed-up files to a "loaner disk" while your disk is being repaired.

Periodically, you should use the COPY command to copy all your files to a backup medium, like floppy disks, getting rid of all unnecessary files. Then reformat your fixed disk, recreate subdirectories, and copy everything you need back to the fixed disk. You should notice an immediate improvement in disk access times, as no files will be fragmented and large blocks of space have been freed up for storing new files. As a side benefit, you have an opportunity to create a more effective tree structure than you had previously. Beginning with DOS 3.2, the XCOPY command was added to provide you with numerous options, including the ability to select a variety of files and/or subdirectories to be copied-an expanded copy command that is a reasonable alternative to BACKUP and RESTORE.

Examples of usage:

C> **RESTORE   A: C:\LOTUS*.*** (restores all files on the LOTUS subdirectory from the backup disks)

C> **restore   a: c:*.doc /s** (restores all files with an extension of .DOC for all subdirectories)

Review Questions for Chapter 6

1. How are files arranged or organized on fixed disks?
2. Why is a constant supply of good electrical power especially important when using fixed disks?
3. What is the purpose of the PARK or SHIPDISK commands?
4. How are subdirectories designated in DOS?
5. What is a DOS path?
6. Why might you want to have relatively short subdirectory names?
7. What is the primary function of the FDISK command?
8. What command allows you to switch from the current subdirectory to another subdirectory?
9. How do you switch to the root directory?

10. How can identical filenames (i.e., FORMAT.COM) exist multiple times on the same disk?
11. What command creates a subdirectory named "DOS" from the root directory?
12. What command creates a subdirectory named "DOS" from the current directory?
13. What is necessary to be able to remove a subdirectory from a disk?
14. If multiple subdirectories are included in a search path, which one is searched first?
15. How are multiple subdirectories specified in the PATH command?
16. What command is used to view the current search path?
17. What command is used to display all subdirectory names on a disk?
18. What command is used to display all subdirectory names and their files on a disk?
19. What kinds of files can be recreated with the RESTORE command?
20. How can subdirectories be restored?

DOS Lab Exercise #6

These exercises do not require a fixed disk system.

1. Make a hierarchy of subdirectories on Drive B according to Figure 6-1 of this text as follows:

    ```
    A> MD B:\WORD
    A> MD B:\WORD\BOOK
    A> MD B:\WORD\MEMO
    A> MD B:\WORD\LTRS
    A> MD B:\LOTUS
    A> MD B:\LOTUS\CURR
    A> MD B:\LOTUS\HIST
    ```

    Did you remember to use the DOS editing keys to assist you?

2. Copy one of the files currently residing on the root directory of Drive B: to each of the seven subdirectories created above.

    Example: **COPY B:LINEDIT.DOC B:\WORD**

112 FIXED DISK CONCEPTS AND COMMANDS

3. Check out your new directory structure by entering:

   A> DIR B: (lists files and directories in root directory)
   A> DIR B:\word (lists all files and directories in \WORD -- the screen should look similar to Figure 6-3)

```
A>dir b:\word

 Volume in drive B is DATADISK
 Directory of  B:\WORD

.            <DIR>        10-04-87   2:23p
..           <DIR>        10-04-87   2:23p
BOOK         <DIR>        10-04-87   2:23p
LTRS         <DIR>        10-04-87   2:23p
LINEDIT  DOC       346    10-04-87   2:27p
MEMO         <DIR>        10-04-87   2:37p
        6 File(s)    229376 bytes free

A>
```

Figure 6-3 Screen Display

   A> TREE   B:/F (lists all files and directories on Drive B -- the screen should look similar to the last part of Figure 6-4)

```
A>tree /f
A>
A>tree b:/f
DIRECTORY PATH LISTING FOR VOLUME DATADISK

Files:           COMMAND .COM
                 TEST    .1
                 READ    .ME
                 TEST    .3
                 TEST    .4
                 TEST1   .DIR
                 TEST2   .DIR
                 TEST3   .DIR
                 LINEDIT .DOC
                 AUTOEXEC.BAT


Path: \WORD

Sub-directories: BOOK
                 LTRS
                 MEMO

Files:           LINEDIT .DOC
```

continued

Figure 6-4 continued

```
Path: \WORD\BOOK
Sub-directories:  None
Files:            LINEDIT .DOC


Path: \WORD\LTRS
Sub-directories:  None
Files:            LINEDIT .DOC


Path: \WORD\MEMO
Sub-directories:  None
Files:            None


Path: \LOTUS
Sub-directories:  CURR
                  HIST
```

```
Files:            LINEDIT .DOC


Path: \LOTUS\CURR
Sub-directories:  None
Files:            LINEDIT .DOC


Path: \LOTUS\HIST
Sub-directories:  None
Files:            LINEDIT .DOC


A>
```

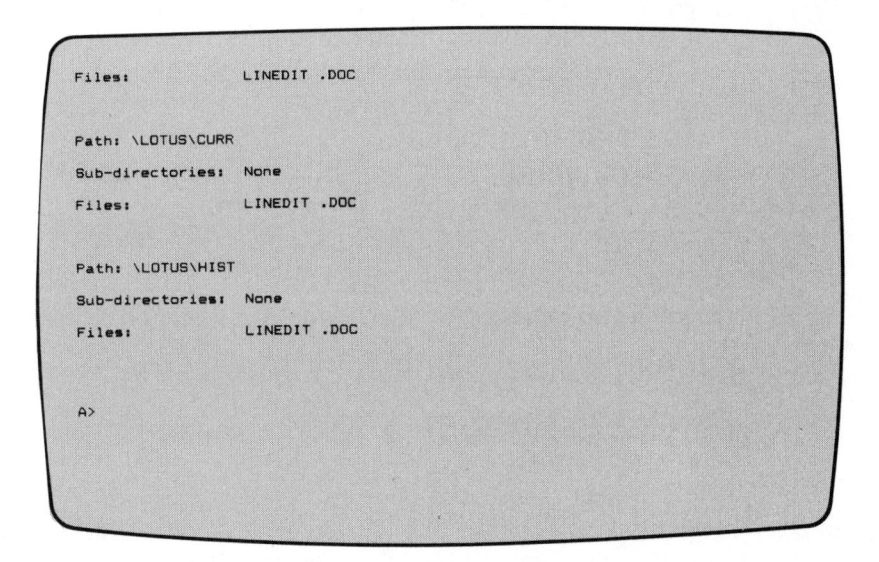

Figure 6-4 Screen Displays

4. Change the default drive to B to facilitate entering commands.

   A> B: (change default drive to B)
   B> CD\WORD\MEMO (make MEMO the current directory)
   B> DIR (test change to desired directory only)
   B> CD (change back to root directory)
   B> DIR (list all files and subdirectories on the root directory of the default drive)

5. Delete the subdirectory named HIST:

   B> DEL   \LOTUS\HIST*.* (delete all files from HIST first)
   B> RD   \LOTUS\HIST (remove HIST subdirectory)
   B> A:TREE   B: (test the removal of HIST by running TREE - external command on Drive A)

6. Set up a path to your DOS external commands:

   B> PATH A: (set path to include Drive A)
   B> TREE B: (test the path, noting that it will find TREE on Drive A after first searching Drive B)

7. Change the system prompt to display the current subdirectory. Then, change to several subdirectories to see the effect:

   B> PROMPT PG
   B> CD\WORD
   B> CD\LOTUS\CURR
   B> CD

This ends lab exercise #6. Remove disks and turn off the computer, if you are finished.

"Practice is the best teacher."

Chapter 7

ADVANCED COMMANDS

ADVANCED DOS COMMANDS
    IF Command (batch file subcommand)
    PRINT Command (external)
    CONFIG.SYS (configuration command file)
    ASSIGN Command (external)
    DEBUG Command (external)

Chapter 7

ADVANCED COMMANDS

Not everyone will need to know all of the more advanced DOS commands. One purpose of this text, however, is to acquaint you with a sampling of the advanced commands. The more you know about its capabilities, the more power and control you will be able to have over DOS.

ADVANCED DOS COMMANDS

This chapter covers only those advanced DOS commands that you are likely to need. These selected commands are:

1) **IF** - gives your batch files flexibility by providing branching capability within a batch file.
2) **PRINT** - allows printing concurrently with the execution of other programs or commands.
3) **CONFIG.SYS** - lets you customize your systems physical configuration and operations.

ADVANCED COMMANDS

4) **VDISK.SYS** - used by CONFIG.SYS to allocate a portion of RAM as a high speed disk device, commonly referred to as RAMdisk.
5) **ANSI.SYS** - a device driver used by CONFIG.SYS to modify the routine keyboard input and monitor output.
6) **ASSIGN** - reroutes disk drive designators to different disk drives.
7) **DEBUG** - allows advanced users to list and/or modify memory locations in RAM and disk files.

Consult your DOS manual for information on the use and operation of any other advanced commands not included here. Appendix A lists all DOS commands with notations regarding those which are not covered in this text.

IF Command (batch file subcommand)

Format: **IF [not] condition command**, where the condition parameter can take on several forms, and the given command will be executed if the condition is true. The NOT condition is evaluated as being true if the condition is false.

The **IF command** gives batch files flexibility of execution by allowing for branching within a batch file depending upon situations that occur during execution. Quite often the command used in the IF statement is a GOTO command that directs DOS to branch out of the normal sequence (that of sequential execution) to another named location of the batch file. In several common situations, the flexibility of the IF statement is quite useful.

If an error has occurred during execution of a previous operation, you may want to skip to the end of the batch file without executing the remainder of the batch file commands. For example:

IF ERRORLEVEL1 GOTO END (If an error has occured, level one or higher, go to END tag)

If a batch file is executed with a missing parameter, you may want to display an appropriate error message and abort the batch file.

IF %1@==@ GOTO ERR (If parameter #1 (%1) is blank (@==@), go to ERR tag)

Additionally, if a file you need in the batch file does not exist, you will probably want to abort any further processing of that batch file. The following batch file segment verifies that a needed file is available before continuing:

```
(beginning of test for condition)
:LOOP
IF EXIST A:%1 GOTO OK
PAUSE  PUT CORRECT DISK IN DRIVE A
GOTO LOOP
:OK
(remaining commands for the batch file follow)
```

If the file specified as the first parameter (%1) cannot be found by DOS, the batch file will pause and direct the user to place the correct disk in Drive A. It will then return to the LOOP tag to continue testing for the correct file. When the appropriate file is located, the If command will branch around the error condition.

As you can see, the IF batch file subcommand gives you a great deal of flexibility to control the proper execution of batch files. Examples of usage of the IF subcommand will be demonstrated throughout the remainder of the text.

PRINT Command (external)

Format: [d:]PRINT [/B:buffersize][/S:timeslice] [d:]filename[.ext]

Normally, when you TYPE or COPY a disk file to the printer, you must wait until all printing is completed before executing another DOS command or program. You can avoid long waits by utilizing the **PRINT command**.

The printer is extremely slow relative to the internal speed of the computer. Thus, a small portion of the computer's resources can be allocated to the print process, while the majority of the resources can be used for other processing at the same time. It is analogous to chewing gum while reading your DOS Manual. Your mind spends relatively little time directing your mouth, concentrating most of your thinking power on reading.

PRINT is a RAM-resident command that gets loaded into the lower end of memory when it is first executed, and stays there until you reboot the system. (Additional discussion of RAM-resident software is included in Appendix B.)

Other programs or commands that you want to run concurrently are loaded into a higher location of main memory. In this way, DOS can execute each program concurrently, allocating a defined slice of time and a buffer size to the PRINT program.

The PRINT command has some limitations, however. It can only be used to print the output of printable files stored on disk. It cannot print the outputs of a program currently running. Unless your application programs, like word processing, can output print files to a disk, the PRINT command will be of limited help. In addition, you cannot change or delete a file while it is being printed with PRINT, nor can you attempt to use the printer for another operation during PRINT. Since the description of the PRINT command in this text does not cover all the options, you may need to refer to your DOS Manual to perform effective concurrent printing. You can also purchase print spooler utility programs that greatly simplify the process of concurrent printing. Commonly used print command options are shown in the examples below.

Examples of usage:

> A>   PRINT   /b:1024/s:64   B:Fed.txt (places FED.TXT from Drive B into a buffer of 1024 bytes and allocates 64 time-slices, so it can print it concurrently with other commands or programs)

> A>   print   fileb.doc (prints FILEB.DOC on the default drive at the same time that other processing operations can be executed, using default values for buffer size of 512 bytes and 8 slices of computer time)

CONFIG.SYS (configuration command file)

Format: (list of special commands to configure the system)

CONFIG.SYS, a special file used in the last stages of the boot process, allows you to specify how your system should operate and be configured. Primarily, CONFIG.SYS allows you to control the way memory is used and to install device driver programs for controlling other devices. It is similar to a batch file in that it is a text file of commands, usually created with EDLIN or the COPY CON command. Here are the configuration commands that you will most likely use.

BREAK = ON used to tell DOS that you want it to check for a Ctrl-C (Ctrl-Break) from the keyboard during each and every disk read or write operation.

BUFFERS = nn where nn is the number of input/output buffers desired to significantly improve disk performance. The default is 2 for the PC-XT and 3 for an AT. Normally, you should set buffers at 10-20. Each buffer uses 512 bytes (1/2 K) of memory. It may require some experimenting to find the most effective buffer size for your system.

FILES = nn where nn is the number of files that can be used at any one time by your programs. The default is 8, but it is recommended to have at least 15, since the number of open files usually includes the hidden files, COMMAND.COM, and several RAM-resident programs. Database applications often need 15 - 20 files open.

DEVICE = x where x represents a particular device driver, i.e., ANSI.SYS, MOUSE.SYS, DRIVER.SYS, or VDISK.SYS. A device driver is a short program that tells DOS how to handle input/output from a given peripheral device (i.e., keyboard, disk, or mouse.) This configuration command must be supplied for each device that requires it installed.

Figure 7-1 shows the commands that typically would be included in a CONFIG.SYS file.

```
BREAK = ON
DEVICE = ANSI.SYS
DEVICE = VDISK.SYS
FILES = 20
BUFFERS = 15
```

Figure 7-1 Sample CONFIG.SYS File

Two of the more common device drivers are VDISK.SYS (RAMDRIVE.SYS in MS-DOS) and ANSI.SYS. VDISK.SYS creates a RAMdisk and ANSI.SYS is an extended screen and keyboard driver. They are both RAM-resident programs in low memory.

VDISK.SYS is a device driver that lets you allocate a portion of main memory (RAM) as an extra disk device, often called **RAMdisk** or "electronic disk." Access speeds in RAM are much faster than those of a fixed disk, so any files loaded into RAMdisk are accessed almost immediately. DOS always creates the RAMdisk drive designator, normally as Drive D.

To install the RAMdisk capability, available with PC-DOS 3.x, you *must* have VDISK.SYS included in your CONFIG.SYS file. If you wanted more than the default of 64K bytes of RAM allocated to the RAMdisk, you can enter a parameter like this:

DEVICE = VDISK.SYS 360 where 360K bytes of RAM would be allocated to RAMdisk (about the size of a floppy disk).

As part of your AUTOEXEC.BAT file, you should copy the various DOS commands, batch files, and programs that you expect to execute most often into the RAMdisk area. For example:

COPY C:\WP\WORD.COM D:

Make sure your path command includes the new RAMdisk drive. For example:

PATH = D:\;C:\DOS;C:\UTIL

It is a dangerous practice to put *data* files on RAMdisk, since valuable data could easily be lost during power failures or surges. Be sure to save any data files you have in RAMdisk to permanent disk storage with the COPY command before turning off the CPU.

ANSI.SYS is an interface between the monitor and DOS, or between the keyboard and DOS. Therefore, ANSI.SYS can be used to change colors on the screen or define the function of keys on the keyboard. By entering a special "escape sequence" of keyboard control codes, you can reassign keys on the keyboard. For example, to change the Alt-F2 key to represent "DIR B:", enter

PROMPT $e[0;105;"Dir B:";13p

The prompt command is used to send an escape code ($e[) to the device driver. This looks like a complicated way to send an escape sequence. However, while in EDLIN or COPY CON, pressing the Esc key aborts the operation. The zero must follow Escape. It allows the enhanced combination keys on the keyboard (Alt, Ctrl, and Shift used in conjunction with the function keys) to be defined. For example, keyboard control code 105 represents Alt-F2. Some of the keyboard control codes are shown in Figure 7-2 below. The text in quotes is the reassigned value and the 13p is required to end the escape sequence with a carriage return.

Control codes	Keyboard Values
84 - 93	Shift-F1 through Shift-F10
94 - 103	Ctrl-F1 through Ctrl-F10
104 - 113	Alt-F1 through Alt-F10

Figure 7-2 ASCII Enhanced Keyboard Control Codes

ASSIGN Command (external)

Format: [d:]ASSIGN d:=d: [d:=d:]

The **ASSIGN command** lets the user reroute a disk drive designator. Some older application programs were designed around the assumption that the program disk would *always* be in Drive A and the data disk would *always* reside in Drive B. However, with the newer fixed disk systems, it is likely that you would want both the programs and data to reside on the fixed disk (Drive C). To execute those older programs, you could utilize the ASSIGN command as follows:

ASSIGN A=C B=C

This command would then reassign both Drive A and Drive B, as required by the program, to your fixed disk. To cancel drive assignments, enter the command ASSIGN without any assignments. A helpful hint: Whenever you use the ASSIGN command, incorporate it into a batch file that executes the program and automatically returns the assignments back to normal. The execution of any subsequent commands would become very confusing if you ever forgot to reset them.

DEBUG Command (external)

Format: [d:]DEBUG   [d:]filename[.ext]

The **DEBUG command** is a machine-level command for snooping around in DOS and making all kinds of subtle modifications. DEBUG can display memory values, modify those values, and view nonlistable disk files. DEBUG is designed for the advanced DOS user, one who doesn't mind diving into the depths of DOS and getting his feet wet. Many novice DOS users have found that working with DEBUG is uncomfortably technical and complicated. Fortunately, whenever an application requires the use of DEBUG, detailed instructions are usually provided for the user. If you know what you are doing, you can use DEBUG to recover lost disk files, edit the COMMAND.COM file, and tell DOS to replace the AUTOEXEC.BAT file with another file for automatic execution.

One of the more useful, yet simple, applications of DEBUG is to view the contents of nonlistable files (files with extensions of COM or EXE). For example, if you entered: **DEBUG A:FORMAT.COM**, you would be able to display the contents of the FORMAT.COM file. Upon entering DEBUG, you would get the DEBUG prompt (-) and it would await your command. Use the DEBUG command "D" to instruct it to display the next 128 bytes from the file. The display is in two parts: the left side displays the data in hexadecimal (base 16) form and the right side shows the character translations. Use the DEBUG command "Q" to exit from (quit) DEBUG. Figure 7-3 shows you what the screen looks like when you use DEBUG to view the first 128 bytes of FORMAT.COM.

```
A>debug a:format.com
-d
0F2B:0100  E9 40 24 43 6F 6E 76 65-72 74 65 64 00 00 00 00   .@$Converted....
0F2B:0110  4D 5A 2B 00 13 00 02 00-20 00 00 00 FF FF 27 00   MZ+..... ......'.
0F2B:0120  00 01 A0 DC 00 00 37 00-1E 00 00 00 01 00 B0 04   ......7.........
0F2B:0130  37 00 B9 04 37 00 00 00-00 00 00 00 00 00 00 00   7...7...........
0F2B:0140  00 00 00 00 00 00 00 00-00 00 00 00 00 00 00 00   ................
0F2B:0150  00 00 00 00 00 00 00 00-00 00 00 00 00 00 00 00   ................
0F2B:0160  00 00 00 00 00 00 00 00-00 00 00 00 00 00 00 00   ................
0F2B:0170  00 00 00 00 00 00 00 00-00 00 00 00 00 00 00 00   ................
-q
A>
```

Figure 7-3 Display Screen

Review Questions for Chapter 7

1. What is the main purpose of the IF statement in a batch file?
2. What does a GOTO statement in a batch file do?
3. How can a batch file detect a missing parameter (i.e., %1)?
4. What is meant by the term "RAM-resident program"?
5. What is the function of a print spooler?
6. What DOS command acts as a print spooler?
7. What is the purpose of the CONFIG.SYS file?
8. How is the CONFIG.SYS file typically created?
9. What is the importance of increasing the default values for the number of buffers and the number of open files in DOS?
10. What is a "device driver"?
11. What device driver is used to create a RAMdisk?
12. Why might it be dangerous to load data files to RAMdisk?
13. What device driver must be loaded to allow you to reassign the ASCII enhanced keys on the keyboard?
14. What benefit could be gained by reassigning special keys?
15. When would you likely need to use the ASSIGN command?
16. How is data displayed with DEBUG?
17. Can batch files be used to redefine DOS commands and create your own commands?
18. What command can be used to display filenames in sequence by filename extension?
19. What command can be used to display filenames in sequence by date created (or last updated)?
20. How is the CONFIG.SYS file loaded by DOS?

DOS Lab Exercise #7

1. Rather than purchasing a utility program to search your fixed disk for a particular filename, you can create your own customized batch file named **PHIND.BAT**. You would not be able to call this file FIND.BAT because entering the batch filename of FIND would cause DOS to execute FIND.COM. Create the batch file as follows:

ECHO OFF (turn echo off)
IF %1@ = = @ GOTO ERROR (if no parameter, branch to ERROR)
CHKDSK /V | FIND "%1" (send all filenames with their path to filter)
GOTO END (unconditional branch to END)
:ERROR (branching location labeled ERROR)
ECHO FILENAME PARAMETER REQUIRED (display error message)
:END (branching location labeled END)

This useful batch file will direct CHKDSK to locate every filename on your fixed disk and pipe it to FIND that will filter out all filenames not containing the string of characters specified by the variable parameter (%1). The IF test allows the batch file to skip over the CHKDSK and FIND operations, if no parameter was included with the batch filename (PHIND) during execution. Figure 7-4 shows you what the screen might look like if you executed PHIND.BAT, first with no parameter, and then with .EXE as a parameter. Note that PHIND.BAT was created on the Drive B, yet was executed with Drive A as the default.

```
A>B:PHIND

A>ECHO OFF
   FILENAME PARAMETER REQUIRED

A>B:PHIND .EXE

A>ECHO OFF
     A:\ATTRIB.EXE
     A:\FIND.EXE
     A:\JOIN.EXE
     A:\SHARE.EXE
     A:\SORT.EXE
     A:\SUBST.EXE

A>
```

Figure 7-4 Display Screen

This batch file could take several minutes to execute if there were hundreds of files to be piped through the FIND filter. However, just knowing you can create such a customized batch file, should make this exercise beneficial.

Use the batch file above to display all files on your DOS disk with "DISK" in the filename. Since CHKDSK will pipe all filenames in upper case letters, the PHIND parameter (DISK) must also be in upper case.

2. Set up another batch file to reassign a special function key. Call this batch file FKEY.BAT and create as follows:

```
REM  BATCH FILE TO REDEFINE A FUNCTION KEY
REM
REM  KEYBOARD CONTROL CODE = 99 (CTRL-F6)
REM  REDEFINITION = "CHKDSK B:"
REM
PROMPT $e[0;99;"chkdsk b:";13p
REM
REM  RUN PROMPT NEXT TO RESTORE SYSTEM PROMPT
```

Once created, execute the batch file and test it by restoring the system prompt and entering Ctrl-F6. You can easily modify this batch file with EDLIN to reassign other function keys. It is limited to a single reassignment per execution, however.

3. Create the following batch file called **SUPERMAT.BAT** that will format a disk with the /S option and automatically copy FORMAT.COM and CHKDSK.COM to the newly formatted disk. This would be a useful program for formatting program floppy disks that are to be bootable and contain the FORMAT and CHKDSK commands. Specific application programs can then be copied onto these bootable disks. If you have a *blank* disk, execute this batch file to see how it works.

```
ECHO OFF
REM  SUPERMAT.BAT USED TO CREATE BOOTABLE DISKS
CLS (to clear screen)
FORMAT  B:/S
COPY  FORMAT.COM  B:
COPY  CHKDSK.COM  B:
DIR B:
ECHO  END OF SUPERMAT
ECHO ON
```

4. The SORT filter may used to sort data in either a text file or directory listing. Since it is able to sort *beginning with* any column you specify, it be-

comes very useful if you have fixed length records to sort. To specify a column, use the /+n option, where n represents the number of the column that you wish to begin sorting. For example, to sort a directory by filename extension, enter:

DIR | SORT /+10 (extensions begin in column 10 of a Directory listing)

This will yield a rather strange looking directory listing since all the heading lines are included in the sort. Create a batch file called **DATEDIR.BAT** that will sort and display a directory in chronological date stamp sequence (i.e., year, month, and day). This becomes a little tricky, since the date stamp is displayed in day, month, and year format (dd-mm-yy). Use the following commands:

ECHO OFF
REM DATEDIR.BAT TO DISPLAY DIR SORTED BY DATE STAMP
DIR %1 | SORT /+27 | SORT /+24 | SORT /+30 | MORE
REM END OF DATEDIR.BAT

To execute this batch file, remember to include the disk drive designator as a parameter when entering the batch filename.

5. Assume for the moment that you have a system with a fixed disk and only one floppy disk. You want to make a backup copy of one of your floppy disks which contains data that is not on your fixed disk. Create a batch file called **C:BUP.BAT** that will facilitate this process if you anticipate performing this type of operation often. The batch file should contain the following statements:

```
REM  BACKUP A FLOPPY DISK ONTO ANOTHER FLOPPY USING
REM  A ONE FLOPPY, ONE FIXED DISK SYSTEM.
REM
MD   C:\TEMP8765
REM  INSERT ORIGINAL FLOPPY IN DRIVE A:
PAUSE
COPY    A:*.*   C:\TEMP8765
REM  INSERT BLANK FLOPPY IN DRIVE A:
PAUSE
FORMAT A:
COPY   C:\TEMP8765\*.*   A:
REM
REM  RESPOND WITH "Y" TO THE "ARE YOU SURE" PROMPT
REM
DEL   C:\TEMP8765\*.*
RD   C:\TEMP8765
REM  END OF BACKUP
DIR   A: /P
```

If you have a fixed disk system, test this batch file to make sure it works. Otherwise, you could use Drive B in place of Drive C to execute this batch file.

6. If you are currently connected on-line to a printer, you can complete this portion of the exercise. Otherwise, just read through it and use your imagination to see how it would execute.

   Without special software, concurrent processing with DOS (version 3.2) is limited to only doing two operations at a time. This can be accomplished in DOS by executing one operation while printing from a print queue. To accomplish this, enter:

   PRINT   B:TEST3.DIR

   Just as soon as the printer begins printing, enter:

   DIR | SORT | MORE

DOS will overlap the executing of both of these operations, using somewhat less time to finish the concurrent processing than if these two commands were not overlapped (executed separately).

END OF LAB EXERCISE #7   Experiment with DEBUG at your own risk!

Appendix A

SUMMARY OF DOS COMMANDS

A
Appendix

SUMMARY OF DOS COMMANDS

PC-DOS Command (MS-DOS equiv.)	Covered in text	Brief Description of Command
APPEND (APPEND)	No	Sets a search path for *data* files.
ASSIGN (ASSIGN)	Yes	Assigns a drive designator to another disk drive.
ATTRIB (ATTRIB)	Yes	Sets/displays attributes of a file.
BACKUP (BACKUP)	Yes	Backs up files from disk.
BREAK (BREAK)	Yes	Sets Ctrl-C (Ctrl-Break) check.
CD (CD)	Yes	Changes directories.
CHKDSK (CHKDSK)	Yes	Scans directory, checks for file fragmentation, fixes errors.
CLS (CLS)	Yes	Clears the screen.
COMMAND (COMMAND)	Yes	Processes *internal* DOS commands.
COMP (FC)	Yes	Compares two files for differences.

APPENDIX A

Command	Resident	Description
COPY (COPY)	Yes	Copies specified files.
CTTY (CTTY)	No	Changes the console to another.
DATE (DATE)	Yes	Displays and sets the system date.
DEL (DEL)	Yes	Deletes (erases) specified files.
DIR (DIR)	Yes	Displays directory entries.
DISKCOMP (DISKCOMP)	Yes	Compares disks.
DISKCOPY (DISKCOPY)	Yes	Makes an exact copy of a disk.
EDLIN (EDLIN)	Yes	Invokes the DOS line editor.
ERASE (ERASE)	Yes	Identical to DELete.
EXE2BIN (EXE2BIN)	No	Converts executable files to binary.
FDISK (FDISK)	Yes	Partitions a fixed disk for DOS.
FIND (FIND)	Yes	Searches for a given string of text.
FORMAT (FORMAT)	Yes	Formats a disk to receive DOS files.
GRAFTABL (GRAFTABL)	No	Loads a table of graphics characters.
GRAPHICS (GRAPHICS)	No	Prepares DOS for printing graphics.
JOIN (JOIN)	No	Joins a disk drive to a pathname.
LABEL (LABEL)	Yes	Labels a disk.
MD (MD)	Yes	Makes a directory.
MODE (MODE)	No	Modifies screen, communications port, or printer port parameters.
MORE (MORE)	Yes	Displays output one screen at a time.
PATH (PATH)	Yes	Sets a *command* search path.
PRINT (PRINT)	Yes	Prints a file concurrently.
PROMPT (PROMPT)	Yes	Assigns a default prompt.
RECOVER (RECOVER)	Yes	Recovers a bad disk or file.
RENAME (RENAME)	Yes	Renames a file.
RESTORE (RESTORE)	Yes	Restores previously backed up files.
RD (RD)	Yes	Removes a directory.

SELECT (SELECT)	No	Selects keyboard/country conventions.
SET (SET)	No	Sets one string value to another.
SHARE (SHARE)	No	Installs file sharing and locking.
SORT (SORT)	Yes	Sorts data forward or backward.
SUBST (SUBST)	No	Substitutes a string for a pathname.
SYS (SYS)	Yes	Transfers DOS system files to a disk.
TIME (TIME)	Yes	Displays and sets the system time.
TREE (TREE)	Yes	Displays directories and filenames.
TYPE (TYPE)	Yes	Displays contents of a file.
VER (VER)	Yes	Displays the DOS version number.
VERIFY (VERIFY)	Yes	Verifies all writes to a disk.
VOL (VOL)	Yes	Displays the disk volume label.
XCOPY (XCOPY)	No	Expanded version of the COPY command.

DOS Batch File Commands:

PC-DOS Command (MS-DOS equiv.)	*Covered in text*	*Brief Description of Command*
ECHO (ECHO)	Yes	Sets batch file echo feature on/off.
FOR (FOR)	No	Subcommand for looping.
GOTO (GOTO)	Yes	Subcommand for branching.
IF (IF)	Yes	Subcommand for conditional branching.
PAUSE (PAUSE)	Yes	Pauses for input in a batch file.
REM (REM)	Yes	Provides for remarks in a batch file.
SHIFT (SHIFT)	No	Increases the number of replaceable parameters in batch file processing.

DOS EDLIN Commands:

PC-DOS Command (MS-DOS equiv.)	Covered in text	Brief Description of Command
# (#)	Yes	Edits a given line.
A (A)	No	Appends lines.
C (C)	Yes	Copies lines.
D (D)	Yes	Deletes lines.
E (E)	Yes	Ends editing and saves the file.
I (I)	Yes	Inserts lines.
L (L)	Yes	Lists lines.
M (M)	Yes	Moves lines.
P (P)	Yes	Pages text (scrolling).
Q (Q)	Yes	Quits editing, aborting the file.
R (R)	Yes	Replaces text in lines.
S (S)	Yes	Searches for text.
T (T)	Yes	Transfers text from other files.
W (W)	No	Writes only part of the file to main memory for editing.

Appendix B

UTILITY SUPPORT PROGRAMS

A Sampling of DOS Utilities for Under $50

A Sampling of DOS Utilities ($50 - $100)

B

Appendix

UTILITY SUPPORT PROGRAMS

Frustration within the confines of DOS is common. This frustration is brought about by misplaced files, awkward commands, and a lack of capabilities. Yet for under $100, users can supplement DOS, thereby surmounting its shortcomings.

There are numerous DOS utility support programs available that make DOS versions 2.0 through 3.2 easier to use and/or extend its capabilities. They are usually menu-driven, so they are relatively user-friendly. Some programs are complete DOS **command shells** that replace DOS commands and their options. These are specifically designed to guide users through the process of executing DOS commands, especially related to the area of disk file management. Other utility support programs extend the capabilities of DOS. In the opinion of many users, these programs provide capabilities and a structure that probably should have been included in DOS in the first place. Some examples are: the ability to recover lost or deleted files, find files more easily, and simpler and faster backup/restore operations.

Some utility support programs are RAM-resident, which means that they stay in low memory (RAM) until you need them, at which time you can call them up with a simple combination of keystrokes, even while you are using another program. These programs are sometimes referred to as "pop-up" windows.

Using RAM-resident software carries some dangers, especially if you are using more than one RAM-resident program.

1. RAM-resident programs can take up valuable space that might be better allocated to the main program.
2. Some programs take over control of the keyboard so tightly that they don't allow you access to your other RAM-resident programs.
3. Loading RAM-resident programs in the wrong sequence can cause your system to lock up. Sometimes, this problem can be resolved by shuffling their order in low memory.

It is not always easy finding a utility program that best meets your specific needs. This appendix lists a sampling of some of the more common and useful utility programs, along with a brief description of each. Because software prices vary significantly depending on time and location of purchase, the DOS utility support programs are listed in two groups: those that typically can be purchased for under $50 (including discount prices), and those that typically cost between $50-100. In addition, software developers are continually improving the features offered and their prices historically drop as sales increase. Therefore, the listings that follow are, at best, to be used as a *guide* for informing you as to what types of general utility support programs are currently available.

A SAMPLING OF DOS UTILITIES FOR UNDER $50

Program Name (company)	RAM-resid.	DOS shell	*Major program features*
CopyIIPC	No	No	Backs up protected software, allows protected programs to be executed from fixed disk.
Cruise Control	Yes	No	Keyboard accelerator, auto-dimmer for the monitor.
dirWORKS ver 2.0	No	Yes	DOS shell with good fixed disk management routines.
Disk Optimizer	No	No	Restores fragmented files, includes a disk analyzer.
DoubleDos	Yes	No	Extensions to DOS, running two partitions concurrently.
Norton Commander	Yes	Yes	DOS Shell
Norton Utilities ver 4	Yes	No	Extensive file management commands, including file recovery.
PC Tools ver 3	Yes	No	Disk file management, file recov., finding files.
SideKick	Yes	No	Desktop organizer, including calculator, calendar, auto-dialer, mini-word processor.
Superkey	Yes	No	Keyboard redefinition, macro generation, keyboard lock.
XTree ver 2	No	Yes	DOS shell & disk management system, excellent graphic display of a tree structure.

A SAMPLING OF DOS UTILITIES ($50-$100)

Program Name (company)	RAM-resid.	DOS shell	Major program features
1dir+	Yes	Yes	DOS shell with numerous disk management routines.
Desqview ver 2.0	Yes	Yes	Multitasking DOS shell
DOS2ools ver 2.2a	No	No	Numerous utility programs to extend DOS, security, unerase, and print spooler.
Fastback	No	No	Friendly and fast backup of fixed disk files.
Nathan's Utilities	Yes	Yes	DOS shell with numerous utilities, disk optimizer.
Microsoft Windows	Yes	Yes	Mouse-directed DOS shell, multitasking, integration.

Index

-A-
ANSI.SYS, 118
ASSIGN command, 118, 123
ATTRIB command, 33, 63, 64
AUTOEXEC.BAT, 24, 26, 79, 80

-B-
BACKUP command, 105, 109
Batch files, 77, 78
   batch processing, 14
   ECHO command, 80, 81
   IF command, 117, 118
   PAUSE command, 80
   REM command, 80
Baud rates, 10
Beep character, 82
BIOS, 21
Bit, 5
Booting the system, 23
Brackets, 46
BREAK command, 47, 121
BUFFERS, 8, 121
Byte, 5

-C-
CD command, 105, 106
Central processing unit (CPU), 4
CHDIR, 106
CHKDSK command, 63, 64
Clock rate, 5
CLS command, 47, 48
Cluster, 34, 65
Command
   external, 32, 63, 105, 108, 109, 119, 123, 124
   internal, 33, 45, 47, 106, 107
   options, 45
   shell, 14
COMMAND.COM, 24, 47, 70
COMP command, 63, 66
Concatenation, 49
CONFIG.SYS, 117, 120
COPY command, 47, 48
   COPY CON, 49
Current line, 85
Cursor, 7
Ctrl-Alt-Del, 23

144 INDEX

–D–

DATE command, 47, 50
DEBUG command, 118, 124
Default
  disk drive, 24, 26
  prompt, 24
DELete command, 47, 50
Delimiter, 46
DEVICE, 121, 122
DIR command, 32, 47, 51
  DIR/P, 32, 53
  DIR/W, 32, 52
Directory
  main, 102
  root, 102
  subdirectory, 102
DISKCOMP command, 63, 67
DISKCOPY command, 63, 67
DOS
  definition, 19, 20
  DOS editing keys, 88
  functions, 20
  MS-DOS, 20
  PC-DOS, 20, 31
  versions, 31, 33, 55, 64

–E–

ECHO command (*see* Batch files)
EDLIN, 77, 85
Enter key, 8
EOF marks, 49
ERASE command (*see* DELete)

–F–

FC command (MS-DOS), 66
FDISK command, 105
File
  backing up, 20
  data, 22

File *(continued)*
  file allocation table (FAT), 22
  file name, 23, 27, 54
  file name extension, 23, 28, 54
  hidden, 23, 65
  program, 22
  saving, 22
  specification, 27
FILES, 121
Filters
  FIND, 63, 67, 83, 85
  MORE, 83
  SORT, 83
FIND (*see* Filters)
Firmware, 14
Fixed disks, 12, 26, 101
Floppy disks, 11, 22, 26
FORMAT command, 34, 56, 63, 68
  FORMAT/S, 35
  FORMAT/V, 35
Formatting, 34
Function keys, 7

–G–

Global characters, 29
GOTO, 118

–H–

Hard disk (*see* Fixed disk)
Hardcopy, 9
Hardware, 4

–I–

IBMBIO, 21, 65, 68, 70
IBMDOS, 65, 68, 70
IF command (*see* Batch files)
Input buffer, 121
Interactive processing, 14
Interface boards, 10

–L–
LABEL command, 33, 63, 68
Lost allocation clusters, 65

–M–
MD command, 105, 107
Megahertz (MHz), 5
Microcomputer, 3
Microprocessor, 4
MKDIR, 107
Modem, 10
Monitor, 9
  composite color, 9
  monochrome, 9
  RGB color, 9
MORE (*see* Filters)
Mouse, 10
MS-DOS, 20

–N–
Numeric keyboard, 7

–O–
Operating system, 19

–P–
Parameters, 45
  replaceable, 78
Partitions, 105
Path, 27
PATH command, 105, 107
PAUSE command (*see* Batch files)
Pause option, 51
Piping, 83, 85
Primary storage, 4
PRINT command, 117, 119
Printers, 9
  draft-quality, 9
  letter-quality, 9
PROMPT command, 47, 53

–R–
RAM, 6, 11, 24, 32
RAMdisk, 118, 122
RAM-resident programs, 119
RD command, 105, 107
Record, 18
RECOVER command, 64, 69
Redirection, 77, 82, 85
REM command (*see* Batch files)
RENAME command, 47, 54
RESTORE command, 105, 108
RMDIR, 107
ROM, 15, 24

–S–
Screen resolution, 9
Sector, 22
Slash, 46
Softcopy, 9
Software, 13
  applications, 13
  integrated, 13
  systems, 14
SORT (*see* Filters)
Standard device names, 27
Storage
  primary, 4
  secondary, 11
String, 18
Subdirectory (*see* Directory)
SYS command, 64, 70

–T–
TIME command, 47, 54
Track, 22
TREE command, 105, 108
TYPE command, 47, 55

–U–
Utility programs, 14

-V-

VDISK.SYS, 118
VER command, 47, 55
VERIFY command, 47, 56
VOL command, 47, 56

-W-

Wide format, 32
Wild card characters, 29
Word, 5